THE EVERYTHING KIDS' BASKETBALL BOOK

4TH EDITION

The all-time greats, legendary teams, today's superstars—and tips on playing like a pro

Bob Schaller

with Coach Dave Harnish

Adams Media
New York London Toronto Sydney New Delhi

PUBLISHER Karen Cooper

MANAGING EDITOR, EVERYTHING® SERIES Lisa Laing

COPY CHIEF Casey Ebert

ASSOCIATE PRODUCTION EDITOR Jo-Anne Duhamel

ACQUISITIONS EDITOR Zander Hatch

DEVELOPMENT EDITOR Zander Hatch

EVERYTHING® SERIES COVER DESIGNER Erin Alexander

Adams Media
An Imprint of Simon & Schuster, Inc.
57 Littlefield Street
Avon, Massachusetts 02322

An Everything® Series Book.
Everything® and everything.com® are registered trademarks of Simon & Schuster, Inc.

This Adams Media trade paperback edition October 2019

ADAMS MEDIA and colophon are trademarks of Simon & Schuster.

For information about special discounts for bulk purchases, please contact Simon & Schuster Special Sales at 1-866-506-1949 or business@simonandschuster.com.

The Simon & Schuster Speakers Bureau can bring authors to your live event. For more information or to book an event contact the Simon & Schuster Speakers Bureau at 1-866-248-3049 or visit our website at www.simonspeakers.com.

Interior illustrations by Kurt Dolber
Puzzles by Beth L. Blair

Manufactured in the United States of America

Printed by LSC Communications, Harrisonburg, VA, U.S.A.
10 9 8 7 6 5 4 3 2 1
September 2019

ISBN 978-1-5072-1252-3
ISBN 978-1-5072-1253-0 (ebook)

Contents

Chapter 7: Hall of Fame 97

Chapter 8: The NBA Finals 105

Chapter 9: College Basketball and March Madness 119

Appendix A: Glossary of Terms 131

Appendix B: Resources 138

Appendix C: Puzzle Answers 139

1 Playing the Game

Basketball: The Basics

Basketball can seem like a very complex game. Maybe you've seen a coach draw a squiggly diagram to show what he wants to do. If you've watched the game on TV, you've probably noticed that the commentators draw lines on the screen during a game to show what happened. How do all of these people know exactly what's going on? Simple! At its core, basketball isn't that hard. It's about hustling on defense and offense, paying attention, taking good shots, and making good passes. If you can do all of those things, you're well on your way to becoming a good basketball player. To be the best you can be, you'll need to focus on fundamentals and practice proper technique.

The goal in playing the game is even simpler: Score more points than your opponent. Some people say the goal is to make more baskets than your opponents, but since some baskets are worth 3 points and others are worth 2—and free throws are worth only 1—that's not always the case.

Basketball is played on a court with a basketball hoop at each end. There are five players for each team on the court at a time. Unlike sports like football, players need to be able to play both offense and defense. They need to be able to make baskets to give their team points, but they also need to be able to stop the other team from making baskets at the other end of the court. To be a good offensive player, you'll need to know how to dribble, pass, rebound, and shoot. On defense, you'll need to know how to rebound, steal, and play all-around good defense, which means never getting lazy.

Basketball is a fun sport because even if you miss the first time you go out and shoot, by the end of an hour or two you'll be making shots fairly often if you pay attention to your form. You can also get pretty good at dribbling in a hurry. Basketball is a sport that many people play because it's easy to learn and there are usually basketball hoops in parks, schools, gyms, and even driveways.

Basketballs vary in size. College and professional players use larger balls than kids. The women's basketball is slightly smaller than the one the men play with. You can usually get a good basketball at your favorite local discount store. If you are using it outside, make sure you get one made out of a synthetic or rubber-like cover rather than the leather ball used for indoor courts; these balls are more durable than the ones you use indoors. Once you have some athletic shoes and a ball, you are ready to get started.

FUN FACTS

Basketball was embraced as a US high school sport in the early 1900s for one reason: It didn't cost much to provide equipment and space to play. Student athletes needed only tennis shoes, T-shirts, and shorts, and schools installed backboards, hoops, and painted lines on playgrounds and in high school gymnasiums.

Players by Position

There are five players on the court at any given time for each team. Here are the players and their roles, and this is for any level, from amateur through college and professional.

Point Guard

Called the "one" spot, the point guard is usually the smallest and/or quickest player on the team. He also acts as the coach on the floor and the quarterback of the team, getting his teammates organized and deciding what to do with the ball. He must be an excellent ball handler and passer who plays with bounce and enthusiasm. Good point guards are usually tough and strong players who love to practice. More often than not, they are confident, competitive, poised, and fearless.

Point guards can be counted on to understand the coach's system and know that games are won on the inside, around the basket. They also realize that scoring is not their top priority. The point guard plays in front of his teammates on both ends of the floor. He is the take-charge person who encourages teammates and gets them to respond. He has

TIP-IN

Basketball shoes have become big business since the introduction of the Air Jordan, a shoe Michael Jordan introduced for Nike. You only need shoes that are comfortable and don't hurt your feet. It's cool to wear what the pros wear, but you'll play your best in shoes that feel good rather than ones that look good or have your favorite player's name on them.

Name That Position

There's a lot of skill involved in being a good basketball player. First, you have to know your position. Someone has forgotten the full names here. Can you fill in the blanks?

_____ guard
(usually the best
scorer on the team)

_____
forward
(usually the
most athletic)

_____ guard
(usually shortest
and fastest)

_____ forward
(usually not as tall
as the center)

_____
(usually tallest
and slowest)

ELEPHANT BALL

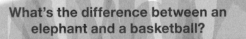

What's the difference between an
elephant and a basketball?

One is big and round and charges through
nets and the other is a basketball!

great court vision and freely gives up the ball to the first open teammate. A point guard must be able to lead the team in assists each season and be able to come through in the clutch by handling the ball in the final moments of a close game. He must be able to make high-pressure free throws if he is fouled in the closing minutes of a tough game. Point guards are rarely the leading scorers on the team since they have other responsibilities, but they should average 10–12 points and at least five assists per game.

Shooting Guard

The shooting guard, or "two," must be a very versatile player. She is usually the bigger of the two guards and the best shooter on the team. She is a scorer who can both take the ball to the basket and make the outside shot with regularity. Shooting guards are expected to be excellent outside shooters to 20 feet. Also known as an off guard, she should be a very good ball handler, capable of rushing the ball up the court on a fast break or ready to take over for the point guard in breaking the opponent's defense and running the offense. The off guard should be the second-best passer on the team and should be capable of playing great defense to stop the other team's shooting guard. A shooting guard must understand what shots the coach wants her to take. She must be willing to take and make a good percentage of the big shots late in the game.

Small Forward

The "three," as it is known, is probably the most athletic position on the team because the small forward must be able to play inside the key area by the basket and shoot from the outside too. Usually the smaller of the two forwards, the small forward must be capable of rebounding and scoring against taller players. He must be able to handle the ball outside on the perimeter against smaller players. This position is

one of the more physically demanding, and the player needs to be both tough and aggressive in rebounding to compensate for lack of size. The ideal small forward should average five to seven rebounds per game and have an excellent jump shot, along with the ability to drive and score in traffic. The small forward requires a player who can run and fill the lane on a fast break. A fast break is when the team gets the ball near their basket and runs toward the other end of the court with the ball, also known as breaking fast up the court. A small forward must also help against presses, which is when a defensive team comes into their opponents' end of the floor to guard them all the way up the court into the offensive end rather than just running back and waiting for the team with the ball to come into their end of the court. The small forward must also be disciplined enough to rebound missed shots. Because of the versatility required to play this position, the small forward often becomes the leading scorer on the team.

Power Forward

This is called the "four" position, usually the tallest or strongest of the two forwards. The power forward is usually a player who likes physical play and has a shooting range of 15 feet. They can be intimidating players and have to play with an attitude that they will out-work and out-hustle their opponents. A true power forward knows that the success of the team depends on his ability to become a dominant force and top rebounder. They should average seven to nine rebounds per game at the college or professional level; they should be one of the two leading rebounders on the team, along with the center. They are the best offensive rebounders on the team, scoring the majority of their points off the offensive board and in the lane, the area in the free-throw box on either side of the basket. You will see players run through the lane with the ball to score or jump through the lane to get rebounds.

Power forwards are the best outlet passers; an outlet pass is thrown by the player who gets the rebound after a missed shot. This outlet pass can result in a "fast break" where the players rush the ball up the court so that the defense on the other team does not have the time to set up properly. Depending on the fast break, they cover defensively on an inside post player. The post is the area on either side of the free-throw line. It's where players who dunk usually get the ball because they are only 5 to 8 feet from the hoop when someone passes them the ball. Power forwards are able to anticipate when a shot will be taken so they can start to the board early to rebound.

Center

This is called the "five" spot. Many people believe that this is the most difficult position to play because of the short reaction time caused by congestion in the lane and the fact that the player must perform offensively with her back to the basket. The center is normally the tallest player on the team and the most effective player with her back to the basket. Strength is a very important part of playing this position. The center needs to be able to muscle her way to a position where she can receive the ball and score even with several players around her.

Good teams try to pass the ball inside on about every fourth pass, so centers should also lead in the number of free-throw attempts. The center must be able to use her body to establish position so her teammates can collapse the defense by getting the ball inside. Shooting range is not particularly important to playing this position, but it's critical for the center to learn the basic post moves and be able to decide when to use each move. The center should rival the power forward for the most number of rebounds. The center is the last line of defense before the basket, and must be willing to help teammates defensively

FUN FACTS

The Los Angeles Sparks selected Stanford forward Nneka Ogwumike as the first overall pick in the 2012 WNBA Draft. Nneka played on the WNBA All-Star Team in 2013, 2014, 2015, 2017, and 2018 and won the WNBA Most Valuable Player award in 2016. She also helped lead the Sparks to win the WNBA Championship in 2016.

WORDS TO KNOW

Blocks

A blocked shot is a ball that is swatted away or knocked down as the player is taking a shot. If the ball is already on its way down toward the hoop when it is blocked, it is called goaltending, and the basket counts even if it does not go in.

by blocking shots or taking a charge on opposing players when they attempt to drive to the basket. A charge is when a defensive player has both feet planted and an offensive player with the ball runs into her. If the defender's feet are not planted firmly in place, she will be called for a "block" or blocking the person with the ball. However, a fast defender can anticipate where the player with the ball is going, get to that place first, and draw the foul on the offensive player.

Offense

If you are going to have an offense, you have to be able to score. To score, you have to be able to make shots. And to get good shots, you need to know how to dribble, pass, and shoot the basketball. Once you know these principles and practice them, you will be able to develop your offensive skills.

Shooting is something you have to practice a lot to get good at. Face the basket when you shoot the ball. Place your feet about a shoulder-width apart, bend your knees slightly, and keep your back straight. Hold the ball in your shooting hand, but position the other hand on the side of the ball to help guide the shot. You shoot the ball more with your fingertips, so you don't want the ball in the palm of your hand when you shoot it. Think about keeping the ball from resting in the palm of your hand and always using your fingertips.

To be a good offensive player, you'll need to master the following types of shots:

- **Jump shot.** Taken from the standing position, you jump as you shoot the ball. Jumping gives you more power and range and helps prevent opposing players from blocking your shot. By jumping, you can shoot over your opponent. The jump shot is the most common type of shot.

- **Set shot.** Taken from the standing position, your feet do not leave the floor. A free throw is considered a set shot.
- **Layup.** This occurs when a player is dribbling very close to the basket, approaching it from the left or right side rather than straight on. You will often use the backboard to bank the ball into the basket.

Passing

Passing is one of the most important parts of the game. You can pass the ball to open players to get better shots or to players who are not being guarded by opponents. You often step forward as you pass to generate power; however, you can also pass while you are standing still if someone is open and you don't need a lot of force to get the ball to him quickly.

When you watch a game, see if you can identify the following types of passes:

- **Chest pass.** The ball is passed from the passer's chest to the receiver's chest.
- **Bounce pass.** The passer throws the ball and it bounces about two-thirds of the way toward the receiver. Typically, the bounce pass takes longer to complete, though it is harder to intercept because defenders usually hold their hands up to block chest passes and shots. The bounce pass is used to throw the ball around defenders.
- **Overhead pass.** Use this type of pass to throw the ball over your defenders; you will use two hands to pass the ball from over your head.
- **Outlet pass.** This type of pass can be thrown to move the ball rapidly up the floor and may be thrown using one arm, baseball style.
- **No-look pass.** This is for advanced players, and is used to keep the opposing player from knowing where you will pass the ball. This is a high-risk pass and should only be

WORDS TO KNOW

Brick
A shot that misses the rim and bounces hard off the backboard. The shot is different from an air ball because an air ball misses everything, whereas the brick hits something—and hits it hard. Players without a good arc to their shots are more likely to shoot bricks. Players who shoot a lot of bricks are called "bricklayers."

Air ball
The term used when the ball is shot, misses the rim, and touches neither the rim nor the backboard. Even though the player missed the basket by a long shot, it is not considered good sportsmanship for crowds to chant "Air ball," especially at a children's game.

Bank shot
Think of bouncing a paper ball off the wall into a trashcan. A bank shot gives you a chance to aim at something you can see on the backboard. A bank shot is also harder to block because the player defending you usually anticipates the shot going toward the rim, not toward a spot on the backboard.

Behind-the-back pass

In a behind-the-back pass, you pass the ball behind your back to a teammate. These are hard to do accurately and are often intercepted, and even your teammates might not be expecting the ball. Learn to do the basic passes well first.

used with coach's approval and once you have thoroughly mastered it and all other passes.

You can also pass off the dribble. Instead of dribbling the ball to yourself, you can push it to one of your teammates. It is similar to a bounce pass, but you won't interrupt your dribble to hold the ball before passing it. It's a hard pass to master, but it catches defenses off-guard because they do not have time to prepare to defend it or intercept the ball.

Dribbling

Quite simply, dribbling means bouncing the ball. It's an important skill to master because you must dribble the ball if you want to walk or run while you have it. To dribble, you push the ball toward the court rather than patting it. This gives you more control while you dribble. The best dribblers can run up and down the court bouncing the ball the whole way.

A good dribbler bounces the ball low to the ground, which makes it more difficult for the defender to steal it. To be a good dribbler, you need to be able to use either hand to dribble. Practice changing hands and changing directions to make it harder for defenders to predict where the ball is going. Some players can dribble behind their backs or between their legs. One key dribbling move is called the crossover. A crossover sounds simple enough: You move the ball from one hand to the other while dribbling. But your defender isn't prepared for the change in direction, which makes it harder for her to stop you or steal the ball.

Practice dribbling until you can do it without looking at the ball. Learn to use your peripheral vision to see the floor. This allows you to focus on looking for open teammates to pass to or a good shot at the basket.

★ FUN FACTS ★

Ever notice how basketball shoes look different from regular tennis shoes? The top on basketball shoes goes up higher to provide ankle support for all the running, jumping, and cutting basketball players do. These shoes are called high-tops because the top goes up higher than standard tennis shoes.

Developing Offensive Skills

Sure, some kids are born bigger, stronger, and with more physical ability than others. But even the great basketball players like Kevin Durant, LeBron James, Michael Jordan, Larry Bird, and Magic Johnson had to practice to get as good as they are. They had to work hard to achieve success. Basketball players are not born; they are made in the driveway and gymnasium and on the playground.

Even though plays can be diagrammed in hundreds of different ways, basketball's simplicity is part of its beauty. A kid who wants to become a better dribbler needs only a basketball and a hard, flat surface. If you want to work on shots from all over, all you need is a ball and a hoop. Conditioning for the sport involves a lot of running, which can be done almost anywhere—outside of the house, please!

To ensure you are on the right track to becoming a successful basketball player, try these:

- Shoot a layup from either side of the basket.
- Dribble the length of the court using either hand. Keep your head up; don't look at the ball.
- Shoot a jump shot from 8 to 12 feet away from the basket after catching a pass.
- Dribble to within 8 to 12 feet of the basket and shoot a shot from there.
- Make a two-handed chest pass, approximately 15 feet, to a moving target.
- Make five out of ten free throws from 12 feet away. Then practice until you can make five out of ten free throws from the regulation 15-foot free-throw line.

WORDS TO KNOW

Double dribble
Double dribbling means you start dribbling, stop, and start dribbling again. This is not allowed, and if you get called for it, you have to turn the ball over to the other team. Don't stop dribbling unless you are ready to shoot or make a pass. Once you stop dribbling, do not even think about dribbling again as an option.

Basketball Position

The proper basketball position is important to master when you first start playing. A proper base position is like the foundation of a house—it holds everything up. A bad base position will cause you problems defending, shooting, and scoring.

What to Do with Your Legs

To get into the proper basketball position, bend your knees, place your feet about shoulder-width apart, and raise your hands to about chest or shoulder level. Getting in this position keeps you balanced. If you are standing straight up, you won't be able to react quickly, whether it's to catch or intercept a pass, break toward a basket, get open, or move to cover an opponent. Having your knees slightly bent allows you to spring into action.

Keeping your feet apart allows you the best balance. You are also ready to take off running. You generally want to have one foot slightly in front of the other foot. This staggered stance allows you a better reaction time.

Your feet are just as important as your arms in basketball. When you are playing defense, you never want to cross one foot over the other when guarding a player. If you do, your opponent can catch you off-stride and change direction on you. For example, if you are moving to your right and you use your left foot to step over your right foot, your opponent will cut to your left and leave you in the dust. By moving your feet in a shuffling manner and never crossing over, you can keep your opponent in front of you and make it harder for her to escape you.

What to Do with Your Arms

Keep your arms close to your chest. This allows your wrists and hands to be in the proper position to catch the ball. You also want to keep your head neither too far forward nor too far backward. Think of it as a line running down your head through the middle of your body to the floor. That's the proper basketball position. If your hands are on your hips or by your side, you will be caught off-guard if a pass or a rebound comes toward you.

Basketball Speed

It's funny, but track stars aren't often great basketball players. You don't have to be a fast runner to be a basketball player. It is more important to be a good player and be quick than to be really fast. You need to move to the right place on the floor rather than just sprint up and down. Knowing where you need to be and staying in the proper basketball position will usually allow you to get to the right place more quickly than someone who is a faster runner than you are. You need to work on your starts and stops, your pivots, and changing direction. These are not difficult things to master, but they take a lot of practice.

First things first: When you change direction, you want to be low and turn your head in the direction you want to go. If you are heading left, take that first step with your left foot; if you are going right, take off with your right foot first.

You need to be able to change direction and stop immediately. The ball doesn't simply go up and down the court, back and forth. Drills that boost your agility will help your balance. If you lose your balance, you are likely to stumble, commit a foul, double dribble, or be out of position. A big part of the game is practicing how to stop quickly and change direction.

When you pivot, you have one foot planted. This is called your pivot foot. You want to be on the ball of your pivot foot to allow you to move around to find a person to pass to or position yourself for a shot. You should learn to pivot on both feet.

Defense

Solid defense isn't as dazzling as offense, and not many defensive plays make the highlight reels. However, defense is just as important to the game as offense. A good defense

can keep your opponent from making baskets, and it's very hard to win if you don't get any points. Defense is a state of mind and attitude. The amount of hustle and sound fundamentals are the most important thing, even more important than natural talent.

Defense Matters

Coaches are known to say that offense wins games, but defense wins championships. There is nothing more important in the game of basketball than being able to keep an opposing team from scoring points. Many players through the years have made their whole career on playing great defense. Some of the greatest defenders don't score a lot, but they have long careers because they are able to keep the other team from scoring.

Being a great rebounder is a way to develop into being a solid defensive player. Being able to steal passes is another way to defend well. Another way is to be able to cover a player who is trying to pass a ball and either prevent him from passing it or force him to throw the ball away.

Defensive Strategies

There are all kinds of defenses that coaches use. The two main ones are the zone defense and man-to-man defense.

In zone defense, the court is divided into zones and each player is responsible for a particular area. For example, a guard might be responsible for an area on the perimeter or out around the free-throw line. If an opponent comes into that area, the guard covers him until he moves out of that particular zone. The same thing goes for near the basket, where forwards and centers will have particular zones.

Man-to-man defense is much simpler, yet much more constant work for defenders. In man-to-man defense, each player is responsible for guarding a specific player on the other team. So wherever that player goes, the defensive player goes too.

Be a Good Defender!

If you want to play good defense in general, you need to have or develop good footwork. It's important that you know which way to face and when and where to turn. A good defender needs to become a little bit of a psychic. You have to think about what you know about basketball and use that to guess when another player might make a pass or take a shot. If you can do this, you can put pressure on your opponent and try to block the shot or pass. Good defenders are so good at pressuring their opponents that sometimes they can force another player to make a bad shot or turn over the ball. You can become a good defender by learning how to position yourself between the basket and an offensive player. That way, when your opponent misses a shot, you get the inside track toward a rebound. You can practice this by having someone shoot baskets and stand near the hoop so you can see how and where the ball comes off the rim.

Basketball Position and Defense

You want to be in the basketball position at all times on defense. You must stay lower than the player you are guarding. If you are standing upright, the player will go around you. You always want your head to be lower than the head of the player you are guarding.

Keep your weight balanced so that you're not leaning too far forward at any time. If your head is lower, your opponent will not be able to charge past you because he will have to lower his head to start that move. This gives you the advantage because you can react before he even thinks of getting past you, and you can continue to remain in front of him.

You should have one foot forward. Your front foot should be on the ball handler's weakest side. If he is right-handed, your left foot should be forward to force him to put the ball in his left hand.

FUN FACTS

Kevin Garnett was voted NBA Defensive Player of the Year in 2008, the same year his Boston Celtics won the championship. Kevin was known for getting rebounds and making big blocks. He managed to be on the All-Star Team more than a dozen times and is also the Minnesota Timberwolves' all-time leading scorer.

Same but Different

Offensive and defensive plays all have special names so the team knows what they're doing. These teams have the same number of plays but not the exact same plays. Can you find the two plays on each court that don't appear on the other team's court?

Court 1:
ALLEY-OOP
BRICK
SET SHOT
JUMP SHOT
PICK AND ROLL
BANK SHOT
SCREENS
BEHIND THE BACK PASS
THREE POINT SHOOTING

Court 2:
SCREENS
DRIBBLE
SET SHOT
THREE POINT SHOOTING
DOUBLE-DRIBBLE
BRICK
JUMP SHOT
ALLEY-OOP
PICK AND ROLL

How did the basketball court get wet?

The players dribbled all over it.

Always position yourself between the ball handler and the basket. If the ball handler gets past you, get your body back in front of him and between him and the basket. Since you don't have the basketball, you should be able to run faster than the player who is dribbling the ball.

When he stops dribbling, attack the player with good basketball stance and keep your hands moving to make it harder for the player to pass. Hopefully, you can create a turnover.

Stand By Your Man

You also want to stay close to your man, in what is commonly called the player's "bubble," an area 2 or 3 feet around the player. This will make him work to get around you. However, if you are too close and bump into him, you will be called for a foul. If you are right on top of him, it makes it easier for him to go past you on your left or right. You want to be in an area close enough to your opponent that you can knock the ball away or deflect a pass attempt, but not so close that you are in danger of bumping into him.

Keeping your hands up while you defend is important. It gives you a chance to knock away a pass or steal the ball off the dribble. Having your hands up also blocks part of your opponent's field of vision. If you are good with your feet and see a pass coming off a dribble, you can shuffle over and reach out with your hands to prevent a pass.

You want to force the ball handler to go in a direction he doesn't want to go by positioning yourself in his path and steering him off course, forcing him to make an unplanned decision or pass.

Even if you are not guarding the ball handler, your job is still important. You want to position yourself to keep the player you are guarding from getting the ball. Keep your hand and arm in the passing lane so you can knock away a pass or force the ball handler to choose someone else to try to pass the ball to.

TIP-IN

When you are guarding a player taller than you, it's more important than ever to be in the right position. You might be faster than the taller player, so when he moves you might be able to stay one step ahead of him and prevent him from receiving a pass.

Fouls

A foul is called when illegal contact is made or a rule is violated. You can be called for a foul if you are on offense or defense, so you always need to be aware of what you can and cannot do. If you are trying to steal the ball and you smack the ball handler's hand, you will be called for a foul. If you run into a defender who is standing in one place and has position (which means he has both feet planted and not moving), you will get whistled for a foul. If you reach over a player's back, push a player, hit a player on the head when you try to block a shot, or jump toward a player and land on him while he is shooting, you will get called for a foul.

That is why being a basketball player with proper position and fundamentals is so important. By following the guidelines, you won't put yourself in a position to commit a foul. Fouls can hurt a team in a few different ways. A team that is called for an offensive foul has to turn the ball over to the other team. They lose a chance to score, and even worse, they give their opponent another chance to put points on the board. Sometimes when a team commits a foul their opponent gets to go to the free-throw line. This happens when a player is fouled as he is shooting or when the team that commits the foul is in the penalty.

Fouls can be bad for individual players because a player fouls out of a game after collecting five or six fouls. In high school and college, players get five fouls; in professional play, they get six. If you foul out, you won't be able to help your team on the court at the end of the game when it might matter the most. Making two or three mistakes early in a game can get you in what is called foul trouble, and your coach might have you sit on the bench so you won't foul out. The best plan is to not foul, to play smart.

WORDS TO KNOW

Fake

A fake is when a player simulates a shot or a move to the basket to get his opponent to think he is going to do one thing, but then he does something else. The fake, if done well, gets the defender off balance or even out of the way and can often draw a foul.

Turnover

The other team gets possession of the ball. Turnovers happen for a number of reasons. If you step out of bounds or commit a foul, you'll have to turn the ball over. Your opponent can also steal the ball from you or intercept a pass. Players and teams who have good fundamentals often commit fewer turnovers.

Rebounding

When you gain possession of the basketball after a missed shot or free throw, you have rebounded the ball. It's one of the most important aspects of the game because most possessions end when a team misses a shot and there is a rebound. There are two kinds of rebounds: offensive and defensive.

Offense and Defense

The offensive rebound comes when your team shoots and you or a teammate get the ball back. The defensive rebound comes when the opponent has shot the ball at the basket and missed and your team recovers the ball. The majority of rebounds go to the defensive side because the defenders usually have better position around the basket as they defend it.

Being a Good Rebounder

Rebounding is a part of the game that affects you both offensively and defensively. If you let the opposing team shoot and miss and get the ball again, they have another chance to put points on the board. If your team misses a shot and does not get the rebound, you've lost an opportunity to score. However, if you get the offensive rebound, you give your team another chance to score.

Rebounding is about body position and tenacity. Six-foot-four forward Charles Barkley averaged more rebounds for his career than 7-foot-1 center Shaquille O'Neal has. While centers do get a lot of the rebounds because they are tall, they still need to get in the right position. A center that stands away from the basket or behind two offensive players who are closer to the rim probably won't get a rebound, no matter how tall she is. Besides, some of the best rebounders end up with more rebounds by positioning themselves correctly and never giving up.

WORDS TO KNOW

In the penalty
After a team has committed a certain number of fouls—four in one quarter in the professional leagues, six in one half for college-level basketball—their opponent gets to shoot free throws for every subsequent foul for the rest of the quarter or half.

Technical foul
A referee can call a technical foul on a player or coach for unsportsmanlike conduct. A second technical foul results in ejection. Technical fouls can also be called for, well, technical reasons, such as trying to call a timeout when a team doesn't have any left. The penalty for drawing a technical foul varies by league.

Flagrant foul
A flagrant foul is called for a particularly hard foul that either injured a player or could have caused a serious injury. If a referee thinks the player committed a flagrant foul on purpose, that player can be thrown out of the game. The opposing team goes to the free-throw line and gets to keep possession of the ball once play resumes.

If you are on the offensive end, your focus should be on getting in front of the defenders, closer to the rim but far enough away from it to get the ball if the shot misses. You don't want to be right under the rim because the only way you will get the ball is if it goes through the hoop, and in that case your team has scored and there's no rebound to be gotten! You want to be where you think the ball is likely to come down, never under the basket.

How to Rebound

The players who get the rebounds either don't have to jump or don't have to jump very high because they are in the right place and the ball actually seems to find them. You must believe that the ball is yours and you are going to do what it takes—within the rules, of course—to get it. That starts with proper positioning near the basket. Offensive rebounds are harder to get because the team on defense usually has two or three players gathered around the basket who are ready to stop you if you try to drive the lane, which means dribbling toward the basket on through the area on either side of the free-throw area. If you are on the offensive end and you see a teammate taking a shot, try to get around your defender, especially if she has given up guarding you, and move into the best position to secure a possible rebound.

What to Do with Your Rebound

Once you get a rebound, bring the ball down close to your chest with your elbows out to each side, which will help you keep your balance and keep the ball from being knocked away or stolen from you. If it is an offensive rebound, you might want to jump right back up to try to score again or pivot and look to pass. If you are in a crowd and can dribble out, you can do that and pass it so your team can set up another play.

Defensive rebounds are really important to your team. If a team gets three or four rebounds every time they have the

TIP-IN

The best rebounding team in NBA history was the 1959–1960 Boston Celtics, who averaged 80.2 rebounds per game. The team to average the fewest rebounds per game was the 1995–1996 Cleveland Cavaliers, who averaged 35.6 rebounds per game.

ball, there's a good chance they'll score every time. You want to give them one chance, if that; you have to protect the basket. Even if you are guarding the player who shoots, you can help with rebounding. When a player shoots the ball, you should move into position to get a rebound or box out your opponent—keeping a player from getting between you and the basket to get a rebound.

You can never work too hard at rebounding. You also want to work smart when getting the proper position. If you don't get the rebound, don't make your situation worse by fouling the player who did get the rebound. Instead, immediately refocus and commit to playing great defense and then double your awareness and effort to get the next rebound.

Fun Games to Sharpen Your Skills

These games are a great way to really hone in on specific basketball skills. You can play some of them by yourself; others work better if you have two, three, four, or more!

H-O-R-S-E

Want to sharpen your skills with a friend? One classic game is H-O-R-S-E, a shot-making game of skill. You take a shot from anywhere on the court. If you make it, your opponent has to make a shot from the same place. If they miss, they get the letter H. Keep playing until one of you ends up with five letters—H-O-R-S-E—at which point that player has lost.

You can do long shots, close shots, free throws, layups, and even trick shots. If you're just beginning or are playing on a team, it's always better to get good at making the standard shots first. If you can make baskets from a variety of places, your coach and teammates can count on you to score a basket if they get the ball to you.

★ FUN FACTS ★

If you are just starting basketball or think H-O-R-S-E is going to take too long, a popular shorter version of the game is P-I-G. But you can also use longer words, too, if you really want to work on your shooting—and spelling—skills!

Around the World

Another game is Around the World. This works best if you play it with one or two others. Start by making a layup, then backing up with two or three shots on the hash marks of the key. The hash marks denote where players stand during free throws, with the first spot reserved for the players from the defending team, and then alternating with offensive and defensive players. There are spots for four players on each side of the free-throw area. To continue doing this drill, once you shoot a free throw, you go to the top of the key to make a three-pointer before closing in toward the hoop again by making shots from the hash marks on the other side of the key. To finish, you make a layup.

Sound too easy? Make it harder by giving yourself only two chances to make a shot from a given place. For example, if you get to the free-throw line and miss, you freeze there while your opponent has a turn. When it's your turn again, a missed shot means you give the ball to your friend; on your next turn, you have to start over at the beginning. The farther you are "around the world," the more devastating the miss.

Knockout or Bump

This game requires two balls and as many players as you can get together. Players line up in a single-file line at any spot on the floor, usually at the foul line or behind the three-point arc. The first two in line each have a ball. The object is to make a shot before the player in front of you makes his.

The first player in line shoots. The second person in line with the ball can shoot only after the player in front releases the ball. If the second player shoots the ball and makes her shot before the player in front of her, then the first player is out.

If a player misses his shot, he is able to rebound and try to put it back in from anywhere on the court. If the first shooter makes her basket first, she passes the ball to the next player in line so he can try to make a basket before the player in front of him. Proceed until there is only one player left.

Twenty-One

The game is played to 21 points. You receive 1 point for a free throw, 2 points from inside the three-point line, and 3 points from behind the three-point line. You can play the game with two or more players.

One player starts with the ball; the others position themselves to try to grab a rebound. The player with the ball shoots a free throw. If she makes it, she gets 1 point and gets the ball back for another free throw. If she makes the second free throw, she racks up another point and gets possession of the ball at the top of the key. She can make a shot from anywhere on the court, but now the other players can play defense. If she makes the shot, she earns more points and goes back to the free-throw line to start the cycle again.

If a player misses a free throw, the ball is considered live, and any player can rebound it. Whoever comes away with the ball has to dribble it past the three-point line before trying to make a shot. If he makes it, it's his turn to go to the free-throw line. The first player to get 21 points is the winner.

PLAY BALL

Netball Is a game that is very similar to basketball but was created just for girls and women to play. How many words can you make out of the letters in N E T B A L L?

Lists of Lists

Basketball fans love lists and statistics. These "Lists of 10" have become scattered. Do you know where they should go? Figure out what group they belong to and write the group number on the line next to the word.

GROUP 1: Sports with the letter B in them
GROUP 2: Sports equipment
GROUP 3: Cities that have hosted the Olympics
GROUP 4: Sports where you don't kick a ball

Innsbruck ____
skip rope ____
water polo ____
badminton ____
wrist guard ____
handball ____
basketball ____
Atlanta ____
Turin ____
bungee jumping ____
swimming ____
goggles ____
tennis ____
powerboating ____
Sydney ____
diving ____
skiing ____
hockey ____

snowboarding ____
ballooning ____
shoulder pads ____
Nagano ____
golf ____
catcher's mitt ____
helmet ____
baseball bat ____
Beijing ____

racquetball ____
knee pads ____
ski pole ____
lacrosse ____
Los Angeles ____
squash ____
ultimate Frisbee ____
T-ball ____
Barcelona ____
flippers ____
Seoul ____
Calgary ____
baseball ____

2

History of the Game

Game On!

Basketball was actually invented by a Canadian teaching in New England. Dr. James Naismith was a physical education teacher and student at a YMCA Training School in Springfield, Massachusetts, in 1891 when he decided he needed to come up with an activity to keep his students in better shape during the long, cold New England winters. He wanted an activity to do in a gymnasium. Though many of his ideas were considered either too physically rough or not suited for indoors (some involved tackling), James took a peach basket and nailed it 10 feet above an indoor track. "Basket ball," as James called it, was born. A soccer ball was used to shoot baskets. At first, each basket was worth 1 point each, so whichever team had the most baskets won.

The first game was played in January 1892. It ended in a 1–0 score. The only point came from a shot taken 25 feet away from the basket. The court was roughly half the size of the present-day standard court. By 1898, the standard rule was that five players from each team could be on the court at a time.

Since a peach basket had a bottom in it, the ball would have to be manually removed each time someone made a basket. To make it easier, James had a hole drilled through the bottom of the basket so a rod could be used to push the ball up and out. Eventually, he figured out that having the entire bottom cut out would work better, though by 1906 the sport had grown so fast that rims with nets were created to shape the game much as it is today.

In James's diaries, recovered by family members in 2006, many were astonished to learn that he based the game of basketball largely on the rules for a childhood game popular in the 1800s called Duck on a Rock, in which a stone was placed on an elevated object, usually a tree stump, with a player from one team guarding it. Players would throw "ducks" (rocks) at the stone to try and knock it off the pedestal. Once the stone

James never played basketball in college—because he had not invented it yet. However, he was a standout athlete at Canada's McGill University as a lacrosse and football player and as a gymnast.

Duck on a Rock

Duck on a Rock was the game that inspired the modern game of basketball. Here are the rules:

One player guards the platform (usually a tree stump or large stone), which has a smaller stone sitting on top of it. The smaller stone is called a drake. The other players toss their stones (known as ducks) at the drake to knock it off. Once the drake is knocked off, players run to retrieve their ducks. If a player is tagged before returning to the throwing line, he becomes the guard. Before the guard tags anyone, she has to pick up a duck at her feet and put the drake back on the platform. Have fun, but be careful how you toss the stones!

No Law of the Jungle

Why are there no fair sports players in the jungle?

Because of all the cheetahs!

The first basket in that first game in 1892 would have been a three-pointer in any league, college or pro, because even the NBA three-point arc is less than 24 feet from the hoop. That means James's first game would have been 3–0 instead of 1–0 if the three-pointer had existed.

was successfully knocked off, the players would run to try to pick up their ducks, but if they were tagged before returning successfully behind the throwing line, they were "it" and had to guard the stone.

Naismith's Rules

James came up with thirteen original rules for his game of basket ball. Some of these have changed since his teams first started playing the game.

1. **Original rule:** Players may throw the ball in any direction using one or both hands.
   Now: That's still true, but once the offensive team brings the ball past halfcourt, the ball cannot be passed into the backcourt.

2. **Original rule:** Players may touch the ball to make it go in any direction, but may not use fists.
   Now: Still true, but the fist rule has been relaxed. Touch passes do not involve using the fist and even blocked shots seldom involve a fist.

3. **Original rule:** Players cannot run with the ball. When you catch the ball, you must stop and throw the ball from that spot. You are allowed a few steps to slow down if you are running when you catch the ball.
   Now: Players cannot hold the ball and run with it, but they are allowed to dribble it up and down the court. A player who holds on to the ball while he runs is called for traveling and the ball is turned over to the other team. However, if a player is streaking toward the basket, catches the ball at a dead run, and only has a step or two until he shoots it, he can usually get away without dribbling it, though many purists say this should not be allowed.

TIP-IN

James's students used a soccer ball for the first basketball games. To grip the ball better, they would rub coal dust on their hands.

4. **Original rule:** Players must hold the ball with their hands; the arms and body cannot be used to hold the ball.
Now: The ball can only be held in the hands or the arms.

5. **Original rule:** Players are not allowed to shoulder, hold, push, trip, or hit each other. The first time a player is called for illegal behavior, it counts as a foul. The second time, the player cannot play until the next basket is scored. If a player meant to injure an opponent, he is ejected from the game and no one is allowed to take his place on the court.
Now: The penalties have changed. Five or six fouls are required to foul out. An intentional or flagrant foul can cause a player to be ejected from the game, though he can be replaced on the floor.

6. **Original rule:** Striking the ball with a fist or breaking rules 3, 4, or 5 counts as a foul.
Now: Players can do touch passes and be creative with passes.

7. **Original rule:** If one side racks up three fouls in a row, the other team is awarded a basket.
Now: This is no longer the case. If a team commits a certain number of fouls, their opponent gets to shoot free throws for each subsequent foul.

8. **Original rule:** A goal is made when the ball is thrown into the basket and stays there. If an opponent moves the basket to prevent a ball from going in, it counts as a goal.
Now: The original basket did not have a hole in it, which is why James wrote that the ball had to stay in the basket to count as a goal. This obviously isn't the case anymore. A goal—now called a basket—is when the ball goes through the net. James's original rule does cover what came to be known as goaltending, meaning the ball cannot be touched when it is on the rim and headed into the basket.

★ **FUN FACTS** ★

While James brought the game of basketball into existence, he remains the only basketball coach ever at the University of Kansas to have a losing career record. He stepped down with a career mark of 55–60.

9. **Original rule:** A ball that goes out of bounds can be thrown back onto the court by the player who touches it first. If two players get to the ball at the same time, the umpire throws the ball back onto the court. A player has 5 seconds to throw the ball; if she goes over, the other team gets the ball. A foul is called if either side delays the game.
   Now: Instead of letting everyone scramble for the ball, the current rule states that the team that touched the ball last before it went out of bounds loses possession of the ball. The five-second rule is still in effect. All inbounds passes must be made within 5 seconds or the other team gets the ball out of bounds. Also, whenever a player has the ball on the court while being guarded, he must pass, shoot, or dribble the ball within 5 seconds or the ball is turned over to the other team.

10. **Original rule:** The umpire calls fouls and keeps track of how many fouls have been made. He can throw players out of the game according to rule 5.
    Now: Most levels of basketball have two or even three referees, and it takes five or six fouls for a player to foul out of a game. The officials do still have the power to eject a player from the game for a flagrant foul.

11. **Original rule:** The referee is in charge of deciding the following areas: when the ball is in play, whether it is in-bounds, which side has possession, whether a basket has been made. The referee is also in charge of the game clock and keeping score.
    Now: Referees and officials still keep track of all of this. There are officials whose entire job is to keep track of the time and the score of the game, so the referees on the floor can concentrate on other things.

12. **Original rule:** The game is made up of two 15-minute halves with a 5-minute halftime.

Now: The college game has halves and the NBA has quarters. The length of the game varies depending on the level of the game—YMCA, college, professional, or another level. The NBA has four 12-minute quarters and college has two 20-minute halves.

13. **Original rule:** The team that makes the most goals wins the game. If the game ends in a tie, the team captains can decide whether to continue the game until another goal is made.

Now: The team with the most points wins. There is no sudden-death overtime where the team that shoots the first basket wins. Instead, teams play an overtime period, and the team with the most points at the end of overtime wins.

★ FUN FACTS ★

Basketball became a medal event at the 1936 Summer Olympics in Berlin, Germany. James was there to hand out the first basketball gold medal—to the United States. He also presented the silver medal to his native Canada and the bronze to Mexico.

Lucky 13

Some people think 13 is an unlucky number, but it wasn't for James Naismith. His 13 rules worked very well for him. Here are some other things that are considered unlucky. Can you spot all 5?

The BAA—The Beginning of the NBA

At the Hotel Commodore in New York on June 6, 1946, a group of basketball team owners met to talk about a league—the Basketball Association of America—they hoped to start. These were men who controlled the sports and entertainment arenas in big cities; today's owners are mostly businessmen.

With World War II over, the owners felt Americans were ready to spend dollars on entertainment and sports. College basketball was already an incredible success, and the owners hoped they could convince some of the college stars to be part of a professional league. On June 11, two conferences were formed: the Western Conference, made up of the Pittsburgh Ironmen, Chicago Stags, Detroit Falcons, St. Louis Bombers, and Cleveland Rebels; and the Eastern Conference, made up of the Boston Celtics, Philadelphia Warriors, Providence Steamrollers, Washington Capitols, New York Knickerbockers, and Toronto Huskies.

The first game was scheduled for November 1, just five months away, and the rules were based largely on those from the college game. However, rather than play two halves, the pro league decided to go with four 12-minute quarters. With timeouts, halftimes, and other time stoppages, the evening entertainment would stretch to 2 hours, something owners

felt was important to their customers. Though zone defenses were prevalent in college, the owners decided that no zone defense would be allowed for at least the first year. They were afraid the zone defense would slow down the game, so they allowed only man-to-man defense.

To get local fans and to keep travel costs down, teams selected players from local colleges. Providence took players from Rhode Island colleges, Knicks' players came from New York, and Pittsburgh looked for players within a 100-mile radius of the city. The only exception was Toronto, which had just one Canadian player among its mostly American roster. The contracts were very modest compared to the multi-million-dollar deals of today.

The first professional basketball game was played in Canada in 1946. The Toronto Huskies hosted the New York Knickerbockers at Maple Leaf Gardens, home of the famous Canadian hockey team the Toronto Maple Leafs.

The opening game had 7,090 fans, and the Knicks won an exciting 68–66 contest. There was no 24-second shot clock, so teams were in no hurry to score, which explains the low point total compared to today's NBA game.

A Competing League

In 1967, the American Basketball Association (ABA) was founded. Like the NBA, it had an Eastern Conference and a Western Conference. The Eastern Conference was made up of the Pittsburgh Pipers, Minnesota Muskies, Indiana Pacers, Kentucky Colonels, and New Jersey Americans. The Western Conference was made up of the New Orleans Buccaneers, Dallas Chaparrals, Denver Rockets, Houston Mavericks, Anaheim Amigos, and Oakland Oaks. The ABA was always struggling financially compared to the NBA. The NBA invited the ABA to

TIP-IN

Three of the most famous sports arenas were commonly called the Garden. The first basketball game was played in Toronto's hockey rink, Maple Leaf Gardens, but NBA fans probably know the current New York Knicks home is Madison Square Garden. The Celtics played in the Boston Garden, which was demolished in 1997 and replaced by the TD Garden.

WORDS TO KNOW

Shot clock
The shot clock for college and pro games is centered on top of the backboard. It starts when a team takes position of the ball and it is not reset until the ball hits the rim on a shot attempt or the clock winds down to zero.

join together, which they did in 1976. This made the ABA franchises more valuable and guaranteed the teams would survive.

CURRENT NBA TEAMS	
Eastern Conference	
Atlantic Division	Boston Celtics • Toronto Raptors • Philadelphia 76ers • Brooklyn Nets • New York Knicks
Central Division	Detroit Pistons • Cleveland Cavaliers • Indiana Pacers • Chicago Bulls • Milwaukee Bucks
Southeast Division	Orlando Magic • Washington Wizards • Atlanta Hawks • Charlotte Hornets • Miami Heat
Western Conference	
Northwest Division	Utah Jazz • Denver Nuggets • Portland Trail Blazers • Minnesota Timberwolves • Oklahoma City Thunder
Pacific Division	L.A. Lakers • Phoenix Suns • Golden State Warriors • Sacramento Kings • L.A. Clippers
Southwest Division	New Orleans Pelicans • San Antonio Spurs • Houston Rockets • Dallas Mavericks • Memphis Grizzlies

Olympic Dream Teams

The Olympics changed forever when professional athletes were allowed to represent their countries. Previously, the Olympic Games had been reserved for amateurs, but the rules changed for the 1992 Olympic Games in Barcelona, when professional athletes were allowed to compete.

1992 Dream Team

The United States chose 12 of the NBA's best athletes to compete in Olympic men's basketball. Ten of the players were later

Do What Coach Says

These 12 players need a makeover. The coach says they can join the team if they dress the way he likes. Look at the following statements and figure out who will be on the team. What fraction of the 12 players will make the cut?

- The players with beards will get on the team.

- The players with feathers in their hats won't get on the team.

- The players with glasses will get on the team.

- The players with polka dots on their shirts will not get on the team.

Around the World

After inventing the game of basketball, Canadian doctor James Naismith lived to see it spread across the globe with the help of the YMCA.

voted among the 50 Greatest Players in NBA History for the NBA's 50th anniversary in 1996. Michael Jordan, Earvin "Magic" Johnson Jr., Larry Bird, Clyde Drexler, Patrick Ewing, David Robinson, John Stockton, Karl Malone, Charles Barkley, Scottie Pippen, Chris Mullin, and Christian Laettner all starred on the team.

The 1992 Dream Team cruised to a 6–0 record in qualifying play in Barcelona. Even in the quarterfinals, Chris scored a team-leading 21 points to help eliminate Puerto Rico 115–77. The semifinals saw a 51-point US win over Lithuania. In the gold medal game, the United States beat Croatia by 32.

1996 Olympics: Atlanta, Georgia

The United States hosted the 1996 Olympics, so a new Dream Team had a chance to compete on their home soil. Charles, Karl, John, Scottie, and David were joined by Shaquille O'Neal, Reggie Miller, Hakeem Olajuwon, Gary Payton, Mitch Richmond, Anfernee "Penny" Hardaway, and Grant Hill. Coached by Hall of Famer Lenny Wilkens, the Americans were once again head and shoulders above the rest. The United States pounded Yugoslavia in the gold medal game 95–69.

2000 Olympics: Sydney, Australia

By 2000, the NBA had more international players among its ranks than ever before, and leagues in other countries were beginning to gain strength. Though the US team had a lot of talent, it was not as dominant as past Dream Teams. Gary returned as the sole Olympic veteran. He was joined by Alonzo Mourning, Kevin Garnett, Vince Carter, Allan Houston, Vin Baker, Antonio McDyess, Steve Smith, Ray Allen, Jason Kidd, Shareef Abdur-Rahim, and Tim Hardaway. Though the 2000 US team was undefeated, five of the eight games were decided by a margin of 15 or fewer points. The American's closest call came in the semifinals, when they squeaked by Lithuania 85–83. They won the gold medal by beating France 85–75.

FUN FACTS

The Dream Team's margin of victory was much smaller in 1996 than in 1992. In 1992, the Dream Team won its games by an average of 44 points. It won its closest game—the gold medal game against Croatia—by 32 points. Compare that to 1996, when the Americans' average margin of victory was 32.3 points.

2004 Olympics: Athens, Greece

In 2004, Hall of Fame coach Larry Brown commanded a team full of young players. Promising up-and-coming stars LeBron James, Carmelo Anthony, Dwyane Wade, Carlos Boozer, Richard Jefferson, Amar'e Stoudemire, and Emeka Okafor joined NBA veterans Tim Duncan, Allen Iverson, Stephon Marbury, Shawn Marion, and Lamar Odom. But the team never really came together.

Puerto Rico beat the Dream Team soundly, 92–73, in the opening game of the Olympics. The United States won close games with Greece and Australia but fell to Lithuania in its fourth game. An easy win over Angola got the US into the medal round, and in the quarterfinals the Dream Team beat Spain 102–94. But in the semifinals, Argentina, a team that focused on playing fundamentally sound team basketball and good defense, beat the US 89–81, eliminating the United States from gold medal competition. The Americans defeated Lithuania in the third-place game to win the bronze medal.

2008 Redeem Team

For the 2008 Olympics in Beijing, China, the United States assembled a team with talent the likes of which hadn't been

TIP-IN

Why don't the best NBA players always win gold medals at the Olympics? Because fundamentals and defense are the keys to international basketball. Also, many teams from other countries play together year-round, while the NBA players practice on the same team for only a few weeks to get ready for the Olympics.

Inflated Basketball

The first time basketball players made money was in 1896. The team couldn't play in their usual space, so they rented a hall, charged admission, and split the profits. They each got $15. That would be the equivalent of $375 today! The amounts on the balls are in 1896 dollars. If $1 is worth 28 times what it was in 1896, how much would the items cost today?

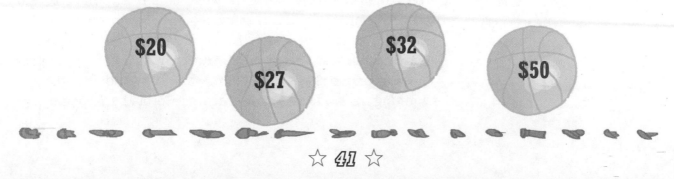

$20 $27 $32 $50

seen since the original 1992 Dream Team. Dubbed the Redeem Team, its players promised to return to the fundamentals that had made the United States so dominant in the past.

James, Wade, Anthony, and Boozer returned, joined by Chris Bosh, Kobe Bryant, Dwight Howard, Jason Kidd, Chris Paul, Tayshaun Prince, Michael Redd, and Deron Williams. Under the direction of Mike Krzyzewski, Duke's legendary Hall of Fame coach, the Redeem Team won every game by double digits, beating Spain in the gold medal game 118–107.

2012 Olympics: London, England

Lebron James led the US Olympic team in 2012, which featured five players returning from the 2008 Olympic team and five from the 2010 World Championship. The team line-up emphasized quickness, speed, and outside shooting.

LeBron James, Carmelo Anthony, Kobe Bryant, Chris Paul, and Deron Williams returned, joined by Kevin Love, Russell Westbrook, Tyson Chandler, Kevin Durant, James Harden, Anthony Davis, and Andre Iguodala. The team went undefeated under returning coach Mike Krzyzewski. They finished the tournament with a perfect 8–0 record, defeating their opponents by an average of 32 points. In a rematch from the 2008 Olympic finals, the United States defeated Spain to capture gold.

2016 Olympics: Rio de Janeiro, Brazil

Only two players returned from the 2012 Olympics team: Carmelo Anthony and Kevin Durant, though they were led by the same head coach, Mike Krzyzewski. Built around size and scoring, Anthony and Durant were joined by Jimmy Butler, DeAndre Jordan, Kyle Lowry, Harrison Barnes, DeMar DeRozan, Kyrie Irving, Klay Thompson, DeMarcus Cousins, Paul George, and Draymond Green. The team again went undefeated, winning the gold medal game against Serbia by 20 points.

3

Great Players of Yesterday

43

The NBA has had many great players since it was started in 1946. One of the fun things for fans to do is argue about who was better, and they will often cite statistics or championships to bolster their argument. Though this is by no means a complete list (the Hall of Fame chapter has more), here are several of the players who contributed to the league's amazing history and built the foundation upon which millions of fans support the league every year.

Centers

Center is a very dominant position. Centers need to be big but agile so they can get the ball, block shots, and grab rebounds before their opponents. They're not usually known for their ability to hit shots, but a few are able to do it all.

Kareem Abdul-Jabbar: Milwaukee, Los Angeles

Kareem Abdul-Jabbar, who was born Ferdinand Lewis Alcindor Jr. but changed his name, was drafted by the Milwaukee Bucks as the first pick in the 1969 draft after a great career at UCLA under legendary coach John Wooden. He won three straight collegiate championships (freshmen were not allowed to play then). Kareem, who was Rookie of the Year, played until age forty-two and holds records for points scored, most NBA Most Valuable Player awards (6), and the most All-Star Games (19). He was able to change the game because even though he was over 7 feet tall, he was still graceful and quick. Defenders were powerless to stop his "skyhook" shot.

Kareem helped his teams win six NBA championships and was chosen to both the 35th and 50th Anniversary All-Time

★ FUN FACTS ★

Kareem gained good reviews for his comedic role in the classic movie *Airplane!,* in which he made several humorous references about playing defense and quips about former teammates.

KAREEM ABDUL-JABBAR

Points	Rebounds	Assists
24.6	11.2	3.6

Teams. A lot of people know Kareem from his championships with the Lakers later in his career, when he played with Magic Johnson. Kareem actually won an NBA title in his second year in the league with the Milwaukee Bucks playing with his talented point guard teammate Oscar Robertson. Kareem was named NBA Finals MVP in that series.

Kareem was traded to the Los Angeles Lakers in 1975 and won another NBA Most Valuable Player award that season. The Lakers became great again and won nine division titles in Kareem's final ten years, during which Kareem helped lead the Lakers to five NBA championship titles.

Tim Duncan: San Antonio

An all-around great player and teammate, Tim Duncan was among the most prolific big men in the modern-day NBA, winning titles both with David Robinson and without him. Tim was the league MVP two times, NBA Finals MVP three times, and NBA Rookie of the Year. He is considered somewhat "old school" because he is very humble. For his jump shots, he often banked the ball off the backboard, which is harder for defenders to stop and is regarded as a more reliable way to make a basket. Tim is just an inch under 7 feet tall, but he can run the floor with most forwards. He was also a very good defensive player. An excellent rebounder and scorer, Tim was the only player to be selected to both the All-NBA and All-Defensive Teams in every one of his first thirteen seasons. He was on the NBA All-Star Team an outstanding fifteen times.

Off the court, Tim founded the Tim Duncan Foundation, which raises money for educational opportunities, youth sports and recreation, and health research. The foundation sometimes gives free tickets to students who show they work hard and have good character. Tim started the organization

FUN FACTS

Kareem changed his name in 1971 after converting from Catholicism to Islam. "Kareem Abdul-Jabbar" means "powerful, noble servant." He was certainly powerful on the court.

TIP-IN

Tim's sister Tricia competed for the US Virgin Islands in swimming at the 1988 Summer Olympics. He might have ended up becoming an Olympic swimmer himself if his community's pool had not been destroyed during Hurricane Hugo in 1989.

TIM DUNCAN

Points	Rebounds	Assists
19.0	10.8	3.0

to give back to the communities that mean the most to him—the US Virgin Islands, where he grew up; North Carolina, where he went to college; and Texas, where he currently lives.

Shaquille O'Neal: Orlando, Los Angeles, Miami, Phoenix, Cleveland, Boston

Shaquille O'Neal was always a winner, leading Los Angeles to three NBA titles in a row and bringing the Miami Heat its first NBA championship along with guard Dwyane Wade. Literally an immovable object at 7 feet 1 inch and 325 pounds, Shaquille was the quintessential big man, dunking and banking in shots after taking passes from his teammates. An occasional actor off the court, Shaq has gotten mixed reviews for his rapping skills and is among the worst free-throw shooters in the game. However, his nearly 24-points-per-game average, coupled with almost 11 rebounds a game and more than 2,700 blocked shots, gave his team a chance to win every time out. He also forced opposing offenses to design game plans that work around his considerable stature. Although Shaq retired from basketball in 2011, he remains relevant, being seen in multiple movies, commercials, and sports broadcasts.

Bill Russell: Boston

As a college player at San Francisco, Bill Russell led his team to two NCAA championships—in 1955 and 1956—though he was forced to miss the final four games of the 1956 NCAA tournament because his college eligibility had expired. Bill still made an important appearance in a championship game in 1956, when he led the US Olympic basketball team to a gold medal at the Olympics in Melbourne, Australia.

★ FUN FACTS ★

Everybody loves a rhyme. Shaq's dominant style of basketball came to be known as a "Shaq attack." When teams fouled Shaq to get him to the free-throw line, you might have heard the term "hack-a-Shaq."

SHAQUILLE O'NEAL

Points	Rebounds	Assists
23.7	10.9	2.5

Court Count

This game has gotten completely out of hand! There are 2 players on the court who don't belong. Can you spot them?

The Fingers of One Hand

On a 10-player team, only 5 players are allowed on the court at any one time.

BILL RUSSELL

Points	Rebounds	Assists
15.1	22.5	4.3

Bill almost did not end up a Boston Celtics player, but NBA coach and general manager Red Auerbach wanted Bill so badly that he traded for the second pick in the draft to get him. Bill was a defensive power, changing the game of basketball by blocking shots. He also had 21,620 rebounds during his career, an average of 22.5 rebounds a game, a huge number that hasn't been matched since. Bill led the league in rebounding four times. He once had 51 rebounds in a single game and twice had 49 rebounds in a game. But above all, Bill was regarded as the ultimate team player and a winner. He led the Celtics to 11 NBA championships in his 13 seasons. Bill is regarded as the most dominant big man in the game, and only Michael Jordan is referred to more often as the game's greatest player. Bill was no 7-foot giant, either; he was 6 feet 9 inches tall.

In the NBA, Bill's greatest foe was Wilt Chamberlain, who put up great offensive numbers, but Bill's team-first attitude led to far more championships than Wilt would ever attain.

Wilt Chamberlain: Philadelphia, San Francisco, Los Angeles

Wilt "The Stilt" Chamberlain was seen as the most powerful offensive player in the game. He was a dominant figure at 7 feet 1 inch tall and 300 pounds. Wilt left the game with several NBA records. He was the only player to score 4,000 points in a season. He scored 100 points for the Philadelphia Warriors in a victory against the Knicks in 1962. He also set an NBA record with 55 rebounds in one game. His offensive numbers were hard to comprehend; Wilt averaged 50.4 points during the 1961–1962 season. His 31,419 points were a record at the time of retirement, though he was later passed by more recent players like LeBron James and Michael Jordan.

Wilt was also a defensive force, leading the league in rebounding 11 of the 14 seasons he played. He could also pass, leading the league in assists in 1967–1968. He was constantly double-teamed and even triple-teamed, and the NBA itself had to change some of the rules to negate Wilt's dominance. Because of Wilt, the NBA came up with the offensive goaltending rule. Once a ball has reached the top of its arc and is headed down into the basket, it is illegal to tip the ball in. Rule changes also widened the lane and made inbounding the basketball more structured to keep Wilt from controlling the entire game. Wilt used to shoot free throws by jumping from the free-throw line and dropping the ball into the hoop until the league changed the rule to say that players must remain behind the foul line.

WILT CHAMBERLAIN		
Points	Rebounds	Assists
30.1	22.9	4.4

Guards

The guard is the quarterback of the offense. The point guard sets up the plays and makes a lot of the key passes, and the shooting guard has a lot of pressure to shoot effectively from the outside and help rebound. These are faster players than the forwards and centers, so they must hurry back on defense. On defense, they do much more running around guarding players than the taller players, who cover a smaller area nearer the basketball hoop.

Michael Jordan: Chicago, Washington

Ask almost anyone who the best NBA player of all time was, and Michael Jordan is usually the first name mentioned. Michael was, above all else, a dominant player and a winner. After he scored 63 points in a playoff game against Larry Bird's Celtics in his second year, Bird described what he had

FUN FACTS

Nobody made more money off the court than Michael—and it wasn't just the Air Jordan shoes. Michael, who starred with Bugs Bunny in the movie *Space Jam*, also represented dozens of other companies including McDonald's, Coca-Cola, Wheaties, Hanes, and Gatorade.

MICHAEL JORDAN

Points	Rebounds	Assists
30.1	6.2	5.3

seen as "God disguised as Michael Jordan." The 6-foot-5-inch Michael was a five-time NBA MVP who redefined the game offensively. He scored seemingly at will, defied gravity with a variety of dunks, and—perhaps most importantly—made all the players around him better. Michael and his teammates in the Chicago Bulls won six NBA titles. Nike built its basketball shoe—the Air Jordan—for Michael. As a player, Michael had few peers; he was too tall for a guard to defend but too fast and too good of a shooter for a forward to try to stop.

A perennial All-Star and MVP, the only question each year often seemed to be who Michael's Chicago Bulls would see in the NBA Finals. The Bulls dynasty was built entirely around Michael, and only Scottie Pippen was considered an All Star–level teammate for Michael. Though he was almost always at his best, Michael was even better in the playoffs when the games were on the line. He shook off double teams—and in one case the flu—to lead his team to NBA championships. Though "His Airness" was known for his high-flying dunks, he was also named the league's best defensive player and was a constant on the All-Defensive Team.

Michael won three NBA titles in a row in 1991, 1992, and 1993. After the 1993 season, he announced he was trading in his high-tops for baseball cleats. Michael played for the Birmingham Barons in the minor leagues before rejoining the Bulls in the middle of the 1994–1995 season.

Michael proved to be just as dominant a player after his baseball stint as he had been before. He led the Bulls to another three-peat, winning the NBA championship in 1996, 1997, and 1998. Michael made his decision to retire a second time in 1999.

Though he will always be known as a Chicago Bulls star, Michael came out of retirement and played two additional seasons (2001–2002 and 2002–2003) for the Washington Wizards before finalizing his retirement once and for all.

Earvin "Magic" Johnson Jr.: Los Angeles

At 6 feet 9 inches, it was hard to imagine Magic Johnson as a point guard. Yet he revolutionized the game with his no-look passes and also pulled down more than seven rebounds a game. Though his shooting skills were never given a lot of respect, he averaged 19.5 points a game during his distinguished career. In addition to his passing repertoire, Magic was a winner, leading Los Angeles to five NBA titles and setting the standard for rivalry with classic matchups with Larry Bird and the Boston Celtics.

Magic's first NBA title came in 1980, his first season. In the Finals, with Kareem Abdul-Jabbar out with an injury, Magic moved to center and pulled his team together to win the championship. He could spin and pass at the same time, throw 40-foot alley-oops to his teammates for dunks, throw really fast and hard passes, and make passes behind his back as he charged toward the hoop. Magic was so deft with his passing that sometimes it wasn't only his opponents who were caught off-guard; his teammates had to get used to being ready for a pass from Magic at even the most unexpected times. Magic passed Oscar Robertson's league-leading assist mark, which was later taken by Utah's John Stockton.

But Magic was the human highlight of passing, and it was just unfathomable to fans—and opponents—that a man so big could pass better than the smallest point guards. Magic was the king of the triple-double—double figures in points, rebounds, and assists. He also won an Olympic gold medal with the original Dream Team in 1992. Magic could dribble with the best point guards of all time and he rebounded like a power forward. He had too many dimensions for opposing defenses to stop him.

TIP-IN

After retiring from the NBA, Magic went into business, opening a series of movie theaters and became a major player in the entertainment industry. He even hosted a short-lived talk show.

MAGIC JOHNSON

Points	Rebounds	Assists
19.5	7.2	11.2

OSCAR ROBERTSON

Points	Rebounds	Assists
25.7	7.5	9.5

Oscar Robertson: Cincinnati, Milwaukee

A 12-time All-Star, Oscar Robertson was NBA MVP in 1964 and led his team to an NBA title in 1971. Oscar, nicknamed "The Big O," was an absolute offensive machine. In the 1961–1962 season, just his second year in the league, he averaged a triple-double with 30.8 points, 12.5 rebounds, and 11.4 assists. It was a feat none of the greats who followed would ever achieve.

Oscar started out with the Cincinnati Royals in the 1960–1961 season and then became a Milwaukee Buck before the 1970–1971 season. During that time he became the top-scoring guard, and only Michael Jordan and Kobe Bryant have passed him. While Oscar's point totals were eye-popping, his passing skills were what left opponents scratching their heads. Oscar was 6 feet 5 inches, the first true "big" guard. So while he had lofty assist totals for even the best point guard, he had rebounding averages that would have made a power forward proud.

Kobe Bryant: Los Angeles

Seldom has a player coming out of high school had such an impact as a guard. A lot of fans don't remember that the Lakers did not draft Kobe Bryant; rather, he was drafted by Charlotte before Lakers general manager Jerry West quickly traded to get him. At just under eighteen-and-a-half years old, Kobe was the youngest player to start an NBA game. He is also the son of former NBA player Joe Bryant.

Kobe had an excellent outside shot, and at 6 feet 6 inches he could drive inside for layups and dunks. Though his 25-plus point average draws a lot of attention, he was also named to the NBA's All-Defensive Team. He teamed with Shaquille O'Neal to lead the Lakers to three consecutive NBA championships. In 2008, without Shaquille, Kobe was named NBA MVP and led his team to the NBA Finals, where the Lakers lost to the Boston Celtics. Bryant impressed the world when he led the Lakers to two consecutive championships in 2009 and 2010, being given the NBA Finals MVP award on both occasions. Since his second year in the league, Bryant has been picked to start in every single All-Star Game in his career, and has been awarded the All-Star MVP award four times.

Isiah Thomas: Detroit

Isiah Thomas was the consummate point guard, handing out nearly 10 assists per game yet scoring almost 20 points per game. He was seldom outplayed by his counterpart. Barely over 6 feet tall, "Zeke," as he was known, could will his team to victories with his drive and competitive nature. He guided his Detroit Pistons to back-to-back NBA championships in 1989 and 1990 and was named NBA Finals MVP in 1990.

During that era, the Detroit Pistons were known as the "Bad Boys." They played a physical brand of basketball that was deplored by many of the new-school athletes but adored by blue-collar Detroit fans. Isiah played in the NBA from 1981–1994 and made the All-Star Team all but his last year in the league. He is only the seventh player to finish with more than 9,000 assists, joining John Stockton, Jason Kidd, Steve Nash, Mark Jackson, Magic Johnson, and Oscar Robertson.

KOBE BRYANT

Points	Rebounds	Assists
25.0	5.2	4.7

FUN FACTS

On the court, Isiah was a winner. Off the court, he's had far less success. Before being dismissed as the New York Knicks coach in 2008, he owned the entire Continental Basketball Association for almost two years, which ended up in bankruptcy.

ISIAH THOMAS

Points	Rebounds	Assists
19.2	3.6	9.3

Forwards

The great forwards of the NBA were often great rebounders and great scorers, and many could dunk the basketball very effectively. Larry Bird revolutionized the position because he brought to it the ability to pass like a point guard. Today, power forwards have to be able to shut down the other team's top offensive players, but they must also be able to score themselves. They are also expected to get a lot of rebounds at both ends of the basketball court.

Larry Bird: Boston

Larry Bird did everything well. He passed, rebounded, shot, played defense—and won. Larry brought out the best in his teammates and the result was three NBA championships. He was always at his best when important games were on the line. Larry was also known for hustling so hard all the time that he would end up jumping over the scorer's table or into the stands to get a loose ball. After having great teams in the 1960s, Boston had struggled in the late 1970s, but Larry changed that, becoming the face of the Celtics from 1979–1991.

With teammates such as Kevin McHale and Robert Parish, the Celtics won ten Atlantic Division titles. Larry was a twelve-time All-Star Team selection. He was also good at the fundamentals, leading the league four times in free-throw percentage. During one streak in his career, Larry made 71 free throws in a row. Though he was not as athletic as Michael Jordan, "Larry Legend" made seemingly impossible shots, ranging from 35-foot jumpers over defenders to layups that seemed to defy the laws of physics. He even rained in jumpers from behind the backboard on occasion.

Larry won a gold medal with the Dream Team in the 1992 Olympics, and even though he talked tough with his opponents, publicly he was understated and even humble. Through his hard work and amazing skills he became a favorite not just in Boston but around the league. From rural French Lick, Indiana, Larry was the original Hoosier. He lived to play basketball and brought his love of basketball into the lives of fans.

TIP-IN

Bobby Knight was Larry's first college coach when Larry went to play at the University of Indiana. But Larry, who was from a small town in Indiana, was overwhelmed by the big campus and dropped out of college after only a few weeks on campus. He took a year off to work and then enrolled at Indiana State University.

LARRY BIRD

Points	Rebounds	Assists
24.3	10.0	6.3

Point Well Taken

The point guard has to be a great ball handler with lots of speed. She has to be ready to attack and think fast. This player is in trouble. Can you see what she's up against?

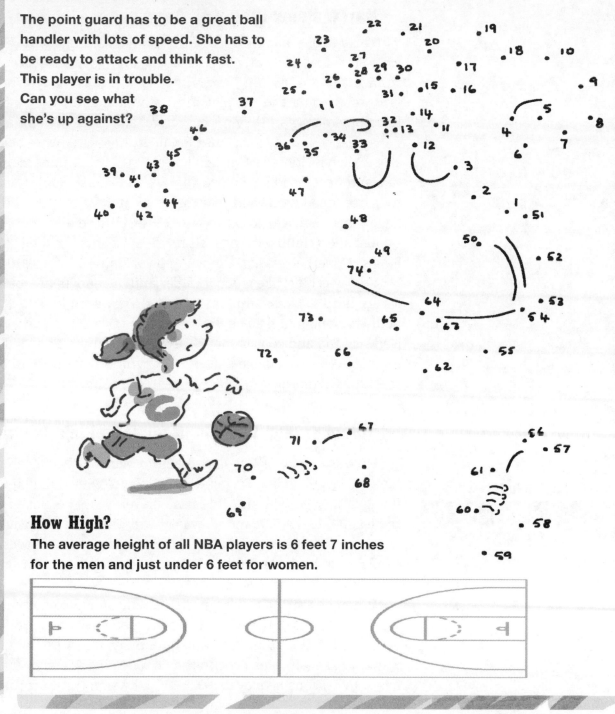

How High?

The average height of all NBA players is 6 feet 7 inches for the men and just under 6 feet for women.

Karl Malone: Utah, Los Angeles

Karl Malone was the face of the Utah Jazz, along with John Stockton, for nearly two decades. Karl played for the Jazz from 1985–2003, earning two NBA MVP awards. Though the Jazz were regulars in the playoffs, without a dominant center to complement Karl they never won an NBA title. When Karl did steer the Jazz into the NBA Finals in 1997, they were beaten by Michael Jordan's Chicago Bulls. Karl's solid fundamentals and unselfish play helped Utah establish itself as a force to be reckoned with each year in the West. Karl went to the Lakers his final year to try to win a title, but the team came up just short, falling to the Pistons in four games in the NBA Finals. Nonetheless, Karl put the "power" in power forward.

Karl was built like a bodybuilder and his opponents found it very hard to block him for rebounds. They even had difficulty stopping him as he drove the ball toward the basket. He was solid and consistent—thus his nickname, "The Mailman." He was a valuable part of the Olympic Dream Team in the 1992 Olympics.

KARL MALONE

Points	Rebounds	Assists
25.0	10.1	3.6

Julius Erving: Virginia, New York, Philadelphia

He was known as "Dr. J," and before Michael Jordan came into the league, Julius Erving was the player with the high-flying dunks. He was an All-Star all eleven years he played in the league, 1977–1987, and he was clearly the most offensively dominating player of his era. Julius was the most respected player of his time and he always conducted himself as an ambassador for the league.

When he started playing professionally, Julius joined the Virginia Squires of the ABA. He was traded to the New York Nets in 1973. When the ABA and NBA merged in 1976, Julius was traded again, this time to the Philadelphia 76ers. In the five ABA seasons he played, 1971–1976, he won three scoring

JULIUS ERVING

Points	Rebounds	Assists
22.0	6.7	3.9

titles, three MVP awards, and two ABA championships. He was NBA MVP in 1981 and led Philadelphia to the NBA title in 1983. Combining both his ABA and NBA statistics, Julius remains one of the top 10 scorers in the history of the game.

At 6 feet 7 inches, Jullius was powerful yet sleek. He glided to the basket for his famous one-handed dunks that brought crowds to their feet. Dr. J's ABA dunk over 7-foot-2-inch Artis Gilmore and 6-foot-9-inch Dan Issel was the highlight of the day.

Dirk Nowitzki: Dallas

Dirk Nowitzki, the 7-foot power forward from Germany, became the face of the Dallas Mavericks' franchise during his time in the NBA. Dirk was also known to stop eating his dinner and let his food get cold just to sign autographs for kids who approached him. What made Dirk such a unique big man is that he could shoot the ball so well from the outside. In his career, he made almost 40 percent of the three-point shots he took. He was named NBA MVP in 2007. Regarded by general managers as the best international player in the league during his career, Nowitzki was with the Mavericks from start to finish, and took them to fifteen playoffs, including their only championship win in 2011. One of the greatest forwards in history, Dirk was named to fourteen All-Star Teams and twelve All-NBA Teams.

DIRK NOWITZKI

Points	Rebounds	Assists
20.7	7.5	2.4

Bounce Back

**Rebounding is a big part of what a forward does in basketball.
There are a lot of words that start with "re." Can you figure these out?**

Re __ __ __
To respond to something

Re __ __ __ __ __ __ __
To place something again

Re __ __ __ __
To go back to where you were

Re __ __ __ __
The device you use to change channels

Re __ __ __ __ __
To lie down

Re __ __ __ __ __
To decorate and fix up again

4

Great Players of Today

Great players from today may or may not end up in the Hall of Fame, but most of these players are leaders for their teams and for the NBA. They inspire a lot of young players to take up the game and fans continue to cheer for them and wear their jerseys. You'll see some of their statistics listed in this chapter, but search online for the most complete, up-to-date information on your favorite players' latest stats.

Centers

Today's great centers are different from their predecessors in one key way: They are as athletic as many of the forwards of the "old" days, and are so physically strong that they can dominate with sheer muscle. These large men are very fast. In many cases, they are built more like bodybuilders than the traditional centers ever were. Gone are the tall, skinny centers who dominated the game decades ago. Today's centers can slam-dunk the ball with enough force to bring down high-tech rims and backboards, yet they can also run as fast as much smaller players.

Nikola Jokić: Denver

Nikola Jokić might be young, but he's already one of the best big men in the league. He's great at getting the ball to his teammates. In the 2018–2019 season, he became the first center to have more than 500 assists in a season since Wilt Chamberlain. And he isn't only great at distributing the ball—he can score and defend as well. He is the third-youngest player in NBA history to have 20 career triple-doubles, after only Magic Johnson and Oscar Robertson. Jokić has been named to one All-NBA team and one All-Star Team, and was part of the 2016 All-Rookie First Team.

NIKOLA JOKIĆ

Points	Rebounds	Assists
16.2	9.6	5.2

Anthony Davis: New Orleans, Los Angeles

After an amazing college basketball career, the multitalented center/forward Anthony Davis was selected first overall in the 2012 NBA Draft by New Orleans. Anthony has made it to the All-Star Team six times and been named to three All-NBA teams. He also brought home gold playing with Team USA in the 2012 Summer Olympics in London. No player is perfect, but Davis shows that he is growing as an athlete with each and every game, with major improvements to his offensive skills. He's a dominant force on both ends of the floor—someone who can block a shot on defense, then get a devastating dunk on the next possession.

ANTHONY DAVIS

Points	Rebounds	Assists
23.7	10.5	2.1

Matching Sets

A lot of players help with charities because they want to give back to their community. Sometimes people give so much that it can get confusing. Can you tell which sports equipment goes with which player?

JOEL EMBIID

Points	Rebounds	Assists
24.3	11.4	3.2

FUN FACTS

Joel Embiid grew up in Yaoundé, Cameroon, where he was discovered by Luc Mbah a Moute, another NBA player who also grew up in Yaoundé. Before learning to play basketball, Embiid wanted to play professional volleyball in Europe.

RUDY GOBERT

Points	Rebounds	Assists
11.1	10.5	1.3

FUN FACTS

Rudy Gobert grew up in France and played for them in the 2016 Olympics. Given his nationality and his ability to block shots, his nickname should come as no surprise: "The Stifle Tower"!

Joel Embiid: Philadelphia

Joel Embiid had a long road to becoming the NBA All-Star he is today. He was born in Cameroon in Africa and didn't play basketball until he was fifteen years old. Even after he was drafted in 2014, he didn't play for two full years because of a broken foot. And then he got injured again a few months into his rookie year! But once Embiid got healthy, he couldn't be stopped.

In his first fully healthy season (2017–2018), he dominated the league. He averaged almost 23 points, 11 rebounds, and 2 blocks a game, showing great skill on both offense and defense. And the next year, he somehow got even better, scoring more points, snagging more rebounds, and blocking more shots than the year before! He was named to both the All-Star Game and the All-NBA Team in his two healthy seasons. In only a couple of years, Embiid has become one of the best big men in the league.

Rudy Gobert: Utah

Rudy Gobert is a giant human being and he uses his stature to be one of the best defensive centers in the NBA. He's 7 feet 1 inch tall, but his arms are almost 8 feet long from one hand to the other! His size makes him really good at grabbing rebounds and blocking shots. In 2017, he went thirty straight games with at least 10 rebounds! Only five other NBA players have done that in the last twenty years. Gobert isn't the best offensive player, but that's okay because his defense can stop the other team from scoring. He was named to the All-NBA Team in 2017 and 2019, and was the 2018 NBA Defensive Player of the Year.

Karl-Anthony Towns: Minnesota

Karl-Anthony Towns is an extremely talented player who was drafted first overall by the Timberwolves in 2015…and Minnesota has definitely not regretted its decision. He's been named to two All-Star Games and one All-NBA Team. He was also the NBA Rookie of the Year in 2016.

A monster on the boards, Towns is great at grabbing rebounds and is already in third place on the Timberwolves' all-time scoring list just four years into his career. He regularly puts up 30+ points and 20+ rebounds.

But he's not just using his size to score and grab rebounds—his basketball fundamentals are also top-notch. He won the NBA Skills Challenge (held on All-Star Weekend in 2016), which is normally dominated by quick guards like Damian Lillard or Patrick Beverley. At the time, he was the tallest, heaviest, and youngest player to ever win.

KARL-ANTHONY TOWNS

Points	Rebounds	Assists
22.3	11.9	2.6

Andre Drummond: Detroit

Andre Drummond is a defensive wizard. He can pull down a rebound against just about anyone and has led the league in rebounding three times. He was the second-fastest player to get to 5,000 rebounds in his career and simply outmuscles and outhustles anyone who tries to get in his way. While he's known for his defense, his offense is pretty good too. He consistently gets double-doubles, leading the league in the stat three times, and twice more coming in a close second. He scored at least 1,000 points, grabbed 1,000 rebounds, blocked 100 shots, and recorded 100 steals in a single season four times, the most in NBA history. Drummond has twice been named an All-Star and once was named to the All-NBA Team.

ANDRE DRUMMOND

Points	Rebounds	Assists
14.1	13.7	1.2

Guards

Today's great NBA guards are stronger and faster than they have ever been. Whereas decades ago, guards were mostly outside shooters, today's guards are taller, but they're just as fast and as agile as their smaller predecessors. Some guards even rebound just as well as many forwards. The guards of today are expected to be a big part of the offense. They must score from anywhere in the offensive end, whether it is driving to the basket for a dunk or shooting a three-pointer.

Chris Paul: New Orleans, Los Angeles, Houston, Oklahoma City

Chris Paul went from nowhere to the center of the NBA universe in a hurry, emerging as one of the top guards in the league. Though his career scoring average is a relatively modest 18 points a game, he averaged more than 21 in the 2007–2008 season, a year in which he led his New Orleans Hornets deep into the playoffs and averaged 24.1 points and 11.6 assists per game. Chris Paul has won the NBA Rookie of the Year award, as well as two Olympic gold medals. He has also been selected to start in nine NBA All-Star Teams, and nine All-Defensive Teams. Chris was traded to the Clippers in 2011 and then to the Rockets in 2017.

The fleet-of-foot 6-footer can distribute the ball like a traditional point guard, but can also drive to the basket with his quick moves. Chris is known for his good court vision and basketball sense.

Family is important to Chris, and when his grandfather passed away unexpectedly during his senior year of high school, he scored 61 points on the day of his grand-

CHRIS PAUL

Points	Rebounds	Assists
18.5	4.5	9.7

father's funeral—1 point for every year of his grandpa's life. If you don't see Chris on the basketball court, look for him in the bowling alley, where he is an elite-level amateur bowler.

Stephen Curry: Golden State

Stephen Curry, 6-foot-3-inch point guard and son of former NBA player Dell Curry, is a six-time NBA All-Star, two-time NBA MVP award winner, and six-time All-NBA player. Steph, as he is known, helped lead his Golden State Warriors to an NBA Championship in 2015 and then led them to an impressive seventy-three wins the next year, the most by any team ever. Though they didn't win the championship that year, he led them back to the NBA Finals in 2017, 2018, and 2019, winning in 2017 and 2018, and establishing the Warriors as an NBA dynasty.

Back in college, during his sophomore year, Curry set the single-season NCAA record for three-pointers. During the 2014–2015 NBA season, he set the NBA record for three-pointers made in a regular season with a highly impressive 286 before demolishing that record the next year, sinking 402 three-pointers. Curry's dominance from beyond the arc has led to a revolution in the sport, as more teams are trying to shoot more three-pointers.

While a lot of young players are trying to copy Curry's three-point skills, it's really his amazing fundamentals that make him as great as he is. His ability to get open (even though everyone is trying to defend him) is unbelievable and his ball-handling skills and passing ability really make the Warriors' offense work.

STEPHEN CURRY

Points	Rebounds	Assists
23.5	4.5	6.6

FUN FACTS

Steph is more known for his sharpshooting skills than powerful dunks. In fact, he couldn't dunk a basketball until he was in college!

RUSSELL WESTBROOK

Points	Rebounds	Assists
23.0	7.0	8.4

TIP-IN

Westbrook was selected in the first round (fourth overall) of the 2008 NBA Draft by the Seattle SuperSonics. Just six days later, he moved to Oklahoma City when the team relocated there and changed its name to the Oklahoma City Thunder.

★ FUN FACTS ★

James Harden is known for his big, bushy beard, which has become popular with Rockets fans. He started growing it in 2009 because he was too lazy to shave and now it's his signature look!

Russell Westbrook: Oklahoma City, Houston

NBA superstar Russell Westbrook is a gift to Oklahoma City. This multitalented player is known for his athleticism, solid rebounding skills, and very impressive boards average of six per game. He is an eight-time All-NBA Team member. Westbrook has represented the United States on their national team twice, winning gold medals in the 2010 FIBA World Championship and the 2012 Olympics. This talented point guard is also a eight-time NBA All-Star.

Westbrook is known as a fierce and fiery competitor who will often push his teammates to be the best they can be. During the 2016–2017 season, Westbrook averaged 31.4 points per game, 10.5 rebounds per game, and 10.4 assists per game, the first player to average a triple-double across the entire season since the great Oscar Robertson fifty-five years earlier. This earned him the NBA MVP award. When Westbrook plays at his best, there are few players more exciting and fun to watch.

James Harden: Oklahoma City, Houston

When you think of the top guards in the league today, James Harden's name will most likely come to mind. Harden was selected with the third overall pick in the 2009 NBA Draft by Oklahoma City and became the first player ever drafted in Oklahoma City Thunder franchise history. In 2012, he was named the NBA Sixth Man of the Year with the Oklahoma City Thunder while leading them to the NBA Finals and is a seven-time All-Star. Harden was traded to Houston prior to the 2012–2013 NBA season. Since then, he has been named to six All-NBA Teams and won the MVP award in 2018. Harden is a two-time member of the United States national basketball team, where he won gold medals in both the 2012 Summer Olympics and 2014 FIBA World Cup.

JAMES HARDEN

Points	Rebounds	Assists
24.3	5.2	6.2

Ben Simmons: Philadelphia

Ben Simmons is a point guard in a center's body. Standing 6 feet 10 inches, he's one of the tallest point guards in NBA history, but he has the quick feet and excellent ball-handling skills that make for a great guard. This combination of size and speed gives him some versatility that not many other players in the league can compete with. Most guards are too small to be great at rebounding because they are often going up against guys who are at least 6 inches taller than them. But thanks to his great height, Simmons can get in and grab the ball before throwing it up the court for a fast-break opportunity.

Simmons is still young, but his skills are already being recognized. He was named to the All-Star Team in just his second year and won the 2018 NBA Rookie of the Year award. He's more of a rebounder and passer than a pure scorer right now, but he can get to the hoop when he needs to. For a young team like the 76ers, he's the perfect point guard, and one who will continue to get better as the years go on.

BEN SIMMONS

Points	Rebounds	Assists
16.4	8.5	7.9

Damian Lillard: Portland

Damian Lillard has been a star since his first season in the league. He was taken sixth overall by the Trail Blazers in 2012 and won every single Western Conference Rookie of the Month award that year. When it came time to vote for the Rookie of the Year, Lillard was the obvious and unanimous choice. Since that season, Lillard has only gotten

DAMIAN LILLARD

Points	Rebounds	Assists
23.5	4.2	6.3

KYRIE IRVING

Points	Rebounds	Assists
22.2	3.6	5.7

better. He's been named to four All-Star Teams and four All-NBA Teams.

Lillard is the perfect guard for the modern NBA. He can hit threes from beyond the arc, score lots of points, and dish out a ton of assists. He was the eighth player to score 10,000 points and get 2,500 assists in his first six years, alongside all-time NBA greats like Larry Bird, Pete Maravich, and Oscar Robertson. He's one of the best shooters in the league, but he is also skilled at controlling the ball and finding his teammates with the perfect pass.

Lillard isn't only a great player on the court; he's a great person off the court too. In 2017, he was given the Magic Johnson Award, which goes to the player who is both great at basketball and great at interacting with fans and the media.

Kyrie Irving: Cleveland, Boston, Brooklyn

After LeBron James left Cleveland for the Heat in 2010, the Cavs were looking for their next star player. They found him with the first overall pick in the next year's draft: Kyrie Irving. Irving quickly became their franchise player. He won the Rookie of the Year award in 2012 and has gone on to be named to the All-Star Game six times. He also won a gold medal at the 2016 Summer Olympics in Rio.

Irving is known for his fast and aggressive style of play and his ability to hit tough game-winning shots. In the 2016 NBA Finals, the Cavaliers had rallied back from being down three games to one to force a Game 7. With just 53 seconds remaining, Irving hit a tough three-pointer to win the game—and the championship—for Cleveland. He was traded to the Celtics in 2017, where he has quickly become a fan favorite before joining the Nets in 2019.

Victor Oladipo: Orlando, Oklahoma City, Indiana

Victor Oladipo's career goes to show that sometimes you have to wait for the right spot on the right team for your talent to shine. Oladipo was drafted second overall by the Magic and had a really good first season with them, finishing second in the Rookie of the Year voting. But over the next few seasons, he didn't do too much. He was even benched at times in Orlando!

In 2016, he was traded to the Thunder, who traded him a year later to the Pacers. That's where his talent came through and he became the star he is. He began to score a lot of points each night and for the first time in his career, he was named to the All-Star Team. He continued his excellent play the next season as well, again being named an All-Star. If you ever feel down about your skill level, think about Oladipo and keep working…you might find you become a star too!

VICTOR OLADIPO

Points	Rebounds	Assists
17.5	4.6	4.0

Forwards

The power forwards of today are the most athletic the game has ever seen. In the past, a 7-footer like the Spurs' LaMarcus Aldridge would always have been a center because he usually would have been the tallest player on the court. But with so many current players 7 feet or taller, height is no longer something altogether unique in the NBA. Power forwards can be strong and powerful, like Karl Malone was, but they can also be tall, lean, and fast, like Kevin Garnett. These players are often better shooters from the outside than their predecessors from decades ago, but they are still counted on to do a lot of rebounding at both ends of the court.

Giannis Antetokounmpo: Milwaukee

One of the best young stars in the game, Giannis Antetokounmpo (pronounced YAHN-iss ah-deh-toh-KOON-boh) is known as "The Greek Freak" for his exciting style of play and the fact that he grew up in Athens, Greece. Giannis often wows his fans and teammates with his wonderful displays of skill and athleticism such as flying down the court on a fast break and dunking from the foul line. He was named to the NBA All-Rookie Second Team in 2014. In the 2016–2017 season, he was named to his first All-Star Game and finished the season leading his Milwaukee Bucks in each of the five major stats (points, rebounds, assists, steals, and blocks). He was also the first NBA player to finish in the top twenty in the league in all five of those categories for a season. He's a three-time All-Star and has been named to three All-NBA Teams.

While he's listed as a power forward, Giannis plays almost every position on the court. At 6 feet 11 inches, he's tall enough to play the center or power forward positions but has the leadership and ball handling skills to play either guard position and the scoring ability to play small forward. Whatever position he plays, Giannis is a great young talent who should control the court for many years to come.

Kevin Durant: Seattle, Oklahoma City, Golden State, Brooklyn

When looking for a well-rounded, versatile basketball star, look no further than Kevin Durant. Kevin Durant, a 6-foot-11 forward, was selected second overall by the Seattle SuperSonics in the 2007 NBA Draft. After his rookie season, the team moved to Oklahoma City and became the Oklahoma City Thunder. Durant helped lead the Thunder to the 2012 NBA Finals, but ended up losing to the Miami Heat in just five games. After joining the Golden State Warriors in 2016, he

GIANNIS ANTETOKOUNMPO

Points	Rebounds	Assists
18.8	8.3	4.1

KEVIN DURANT

Points	Rebounds	Assists
27.2	7.1	4.1

returned to the Finals three times, winning and being named NBA Finals MVP twice. Durant has won two Olympic gold medals, an NBA MVP award, four NBA scoring titles, and the NBA Rookie of the Year award. He has also been selected to nine All-NBA Teams and ten All-Star Teams. Kevin is one of three players in the NBA to average over 20 points per game while still a teenager. Kevin was injured in the 2019 NBA Finals, but he still signed a big contract to join Kyrie Irving in Brooklyn upon recovery.

Blake Griffin: Los Angeles, Detroit

Blake played really great college basketball for the Oklahoma Sooners before the L.A. Clippers drafted him first overall in 2009. During the final preseason game that year, Blake broke his left kneecap, had to have surgery, and missed the entire 2009–2010 season. Griffin made his NBA debut as a rookie the following season, in which he was selected as an All-Star, won the NBA Slam Dunk Contest, and was named the NBA Rookie of the Year. Griffin is a six-time NBA All-Star and a five-time All-NBA selection. In early 2018, Blake was traded to the Detroit Pistons, where he joined Andre Drummond to form a powerful big man pair.

BLAKE GRIFFIN

Points	Rebounds	Assists
21.9	9.0	4.5

LeBron James: Cleveland, Miami, Los Angeles

Few players have come into the league with as much hype and pressure as LeBron "King" James, who was drafted first overall to rescue his hometown team, the Cleveland Cavaliers, from years of mediocrity. LeBron took the team to the NBA Finals, but at that point, did not win the crown that would fit his nickname so well.

He is one of the most dominant players in the game. At 6 feet 8 inches and 250 pounds, LeBron can dribble and

TIP-IN

LeBron is arguably the most celebrated individual player since Michael Jordan—who was drafted by the Chicago Bulls the year LeBron was born. LeBron signed a $90 million contract with Nike before he even started his playing career.

Score!

This scorekeeper is having trouble with numbers and letters. Can you help him unscramble the strings of letters here? Only one of them has all the letters to spell **BASKETBALL SCORE.**

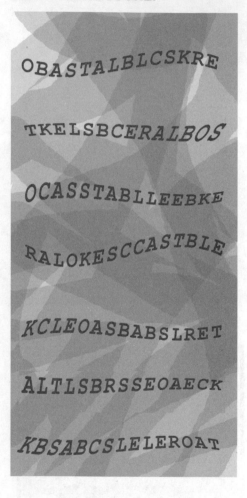

OBASTALBLCSKRE

TKELSBCERALBOS

OCASSTABLLEEBKE

RALOKESCCASTBLE

KCLEOASBABSLRET

ALTLSBRSSEOAECK

KBSABCSLELEROAT

LEBRON JAMES

Points	Rebounds	Assists
27.2	7.4	7.2

pass like a guard but can also drive to the basket against taller defenders to dunk, score a layup, or draw a foul. By drawing so many defenders to himself, LeBron has been able to dish out almost as many assists per game as rebounds.

In 2010, LeBron "took his talents" to the Miami Heat. In his first season in Miami, the Heat reached the Finals but lost to the Dallas Mavericks. After that the team took the whole league by storm. James won his first championship in 2012 when Miami defeated the Oklahoma City Thunder. In 2013, he led the Heat on a twenty-seven-game winning streak, the second longest in league history. Miami also won its second consecutive title that year.

In 2014, LeBron surprised everybody by rejoining the Cavaliers and leading them to a championship in 2016. James has three NBA championships, four MVP awards, three MVP Finals awards, two Olympic gold medals, a Rookie of the Year award, and an NBA scoring title. Appearing on fifteen All-Star Teams, fifteen All-NBA teams, and six NBA All-Defensive Teams, LeBron has a career average of 27 points a game and is the Cavs' all-time leading scorer. In 2018, LeBron again left Cleveland, heading west to Hollywood to join the Los Angeles Lakers.

Off the court, LeBron has been ranked as one of America's most influential and popular athletes, currently and historically. In 2015, James appeared in the movie *Trainwreck* with Amy Schumer and Bill Hader. He has also been the subject of books, documentaries, TV commercials, and he has hosted the ESPY Awards and *Saturday Night Live*.

Opposites Attract

One of the first great players of basketball—in fact, he was called Mr. Basketball—was George Mikan. His training regimen included shadow boxing, rope-skipping, and ballet! Sometimes things fit together perfectly even when they don't look like they should. Can you match these words with their opposite?

AVERAGE	MINOR
PLAYER	AMATEUR
PROFESSIONAL	PULL
PUSH	WALK
BEST	LOSE
WIN	WORKER
TALL	SHORT
MAJOR	WORST
RUN	EXTRAORDINARY

Major Milestone

In 1950, Earl Lloyd became a member of the Washington Capitols. He was the first African American to play in the NBA.

PAUL GEORGE

Points	Rebounds	Assists
19.8	6.4	3.3

KAWHI LEONARD

Points	Rebounds	Assists
17.7	6.3	2.4

Paul George: Indiana, Oklahoma City, Los Angeles

Paul George is a great example of someone working hard to get better at basketball. He struggled in his first year in the NBA, so he trained hard before the next season to improve his ball-handling skills. The next year, he became one of the best offensive players in the game and was selected to his first of six All-Star Game appearances. He also won Most Improved Player. He continued to play great the next season, but then faced a setback when he broke his leg before the 2014 season. He worked hard to come back from the injury and became an All-Star again the next season before helping Team USA win gold in Rio de Janeiro.

Over the next few years, Paul George became one of the best players in the league. In 2018, he finished in the top three for the MVP award. Later that year, he and Kawhi Leonard decided to team up on the Los Angeles Clippers to create a dynamic duo that can rival any team.

Kawhi Leonard: San Antonio, Toronto, Los Angeles

Just as Tim Duncan became a star for the San Antonio Spurs with David Robinson, Kawhi Leonard blossomed after learning from Duncan. Leonard first rose to prominence in the 2013 NBA Finals against the Miami Heat, where he averaged 14.6 points and a whopping 11.1 rebounds per game despite losing the series. The next year, he went back to the Finals against Miami and played even better, averaging 17.8 points, 6.4 rebounds, and 1.2 blocks per game and winning the Finals MVP award. He became the third-youngest player to win the award, after only Magic Johnson. After that, Leonard became a defensive nightmare for other teams, winning the NBA Defensive Player of

the Year in both 2015 and 2016, being selected to three All-NBA teams, and playing in three All-Star games. In 2018, he left the Spurs and joined the Toronto Raptors, whom he led to an NBA Championship, and with whom he won his second Finals MVP award.

After winning the championship, Leonard became a free agent, meaning he could choose to play wherever he wanted. He chose to play for the Los Angeles Clippers, who also traded for Paul George, forming one of the best pairs of forwards in the NBA.

Jimmy Butler: Chicago, Minnesota, Philadelphia, Miami

Jimmy Butler was selected late in the first round of the NBA draft and wasn't expected to be much more than a role player in the league. Well, he has certainly proven everybody wrong because he is now one of the game's best two-way players. He regularly leads his team in points and assists each year and he's a shutdown defender, having been named to the NBA All-Defensive team four times. He's also a four-time All-Star and two-time All-NBA player.

He started off playing for the Chicago Bulls, where he led the team to five playoff berths in six years. He was traded to the Timberwolves in 2017 and then to the 76ers in 2018. Along with Ben Simmons and Joel Embiid, he helped turn the 76ers into one of the most talented and exciting teams in the league. After the season, Jimmy joined the Miami Heat to once again be the star of his own team.

JIMMY BUTLER

Points	Rebounds	Assists
16.7	4.9	3.5

Klay Thompson: Golden State

Klay Thompson and Steph Curry: The Splash Brothers. Just like his teammate and friend Steph Curry, Klay Thompson is an elite three-point shooter and a driving force behind

KLAY THOMPSON

Points	Rebounds	Assists
19.5	3.5	2.3

the Warriors dynasty. Thompson once hit 14 three-pointers in one game, the most of any player in all of NBA history. He's also known for his high-quality defense. While he might not get as many rebounds as some of his taller teammates, his size at the guard position allows him to defend other guards and make it tough for them to score. He's been named to the All-Star Team five times, twice been put on the All-NBA Team, and helped Team USA win the gold medal at the 2016 Summer Olympics in Rio.

Draymond Green: Golden State

Draymond Green doesn't score many points—he lets his teammates, like Steph Curry and Klay Thompson, handle that. What makes Green a star is his defense and his passing. He's one of the few players in the NBA who's capable of guarding any opponent, from quick point guards to powerful centers. This gives the Warriors the flexibility to put their best players out on the court and not have to worry about who's covering the opponents on the other end. Green can do it!

He's also a great ball handler and passer for a power forward. The Warriors' offense is built around ball movement, so Green's passing skills help the offense work, even if he's not putting the ball in the hoop. He's been named to three All-Star Games, two All-NBA Teams, and four NBA All-Defensive Teams, and won the NBA Defensive Player of the Year.

DRAYMOND GREEN		
Points	Rebounds	Assists
9.1	6.9	4.9

5

Women's
Basketball

College Women's Basketball

In 1892, the year after Dr. James Naismith invented what we know to be basketball, the first game of women's basketball was played. Women's college basketball began in 1893 with teams starting at Iowa State College, Carleton, Mount Holyoke, and Tulane.

In 1896, Stanford played the University of California at Berkeley in the first women's intercollegiate game, with Stanford winning 2–1. Rather than the eventual 5-on-5 format familiar to current fans, that game was played 9-on-9. The women's game has come a long way since then.

Title IX and the 1970s

The 1970s were a critical period of growth for women's college basketball. The sport had languished in the shadows of prominent men's programs because the men tended to get more funding. In the 1970s, the International Olympic Committee added women's basketball as a medal sport, and it debuted to immense popularity at the 1976 Olympic Games.

The landscape changed for college women's sports, including basketball, when Congress passed Title IX in 1972. Title IX was designed to make sure that women's sports received just as much funding as men's sports. If a school offers a sport for men, it must also offer one for women. It also evened out scholarships for men's and women's teams, which was important for women's basketball programs. According to NCAA figures, participation in women's sports increased by roughly 400 percent in the thirty-plus years since Title IX was enacted.

Women's NCAA Basketball Today

The NCAA began its women's NCAA basketball tournament in 1982, and Louisiana Tech beat Cheyney State in the final game. There were thirty-two teams in the field the first four years, forty teams from 1986 to 1988, and forty-eight

★ FUN FACTS ★

In 2009, Pat Summitt picked up her 1,000th career win as a college women's coach, becoming the coach with the most wins in women's basketball—college and professional. She finished her career with 1,098 career wins in 1,306 games.

teams from 1989 to 1993. In 1994, it expanded to sixty-four teams, just like the men's tournament. And like the men's tournament, those teams are chosen through a mixture of conference champions and teams that receive invitations.

Tennessee, led by Hall of Fame coach Pat Summitt, and the University of Connecticut, led by coach Geno Auriemma, became powerhouses in the sport. Tennessee won three titles in a row from 1996–1998. Connecticut won four of five NCAA championships from 2000–2004. Tennessee won back-to-back titles in 2007 and 2008. Connecticut would go on to win the NCAA championship in 2009, 2010, 2013, 2014, 2015, and 2016.

The women's NCAA tournament still has fewer viewers than men, but it has drawn impressive attendance and has TV contracts that support it financially and promote the sport in millions of homes each year. The creation of the WNBA also boosted the college women's game.

The WNBA

The Women's National Basketball Association was formed in 1996 by the NBA. The first WNBA games were played in June 1997. The Houston Comets quickly emerged as a dominant team in the new league. Sheryl Swoopes and Cynthia Cooper—the WNBA's first Most Valuable Player—helped the Comets win the first WNBA title. In 2001, Lisa Leslie of the Los Angeles Sparks became the first player to capture all three MVP awards in the same season (regular season, All-Star, and Championship MVP honors).

Women's leagues had failed in the past, in part because they could not get deals with major TV networks to bring in money. But the WNBA had contracts with NBC, ESPN, and Lifetime Television. The WNBA season starts after the NBA season and runs through the summer, so basketball fans can watch their favorite game all year long.

FUN FACTS

While the NBA has 12-minute quarters, the WNBA has 10-minute quarters. The women's basketball is 28.5 inches around—an inch smaller in diameter than the basketball used by the men. After starting with a 30-second shot clock, the WNBA switched to a 24-second shot clock, which is the same as the NBA.

TIP-IN

Women's basketball did not become an Olympic sport until the 1976 Games in Montreal. The United States women lost in the gold medal game to the Soviet Union, leaving America with a silver medal. The bronze went to Bulgaria.

Three's a Charm

On March 21, 1893, the first women's collegiate game was played at Smith College in Northampton, Massachusetts. The physical education teacher, Senda Berenson, must have liked the number 3. There were 3 zones with 3 players allowed in each zone. Each player could hold the ball for 3 seconds and dribble 3 times before passing.

If the ball was passed 5 times in one play, what is the maximum number of times it could be dribbled?

LADIES ONLY!
In 1893, it was considered inappropriate for men to watch women playing a sport such as basketball, so all the doors to the gym were locked for the first game at Smith College.

Eight teams were part of the WNBA's first season. The Eastern Conference had the Charlotte Sting, Cleveland Rockers, Houston Comets, and New York Liberty. The Western Conference had the Los Angeles Sparks, Phoenix Mercury, Sacramento Monarchs, and Utah Starzz.

Teams no longer play in Charlotte, Cleveland, Houston, Sacramento, or Utah, but the league has expanded to twelve teams. The Eastern Conference includes the Connecticut Sun, Indiana Fever, New York Liberty, Washington Mystics, Chicago Sky, and Atlanta Dream; the Western Conference includes the Las Vegas Aces, Seattle Storm, Los Angeles Sparks, Minnesota Lynx, Dallas Wings, and Phoenix Mercury.

FUN FACTS

In 2009, Courtney Paris, a standout All-American center at the University of Oklahoma, promised to pay the school back every cent from her four-year scholarship if the team didn't win its first NCAA championship. The Sooners lost to Louisville by 2 points in the Final Four, but Oklahoma wouldn't take any money from Courtney. Courtney was drafted by Sacramento in the first round, and said she'll find another way to give back to the Oklahoma community.

Great Players

Though the women's league does not get as much media attendance or media coverage as the men's league, the players practice just as hard and the fundamentals in the women's leagues, both in college and professional, can be superior to the men's game. You don't hear as much about individual players in the women's league—the team concept is so strong that it cannot be undervalued. Nevertheless, here are some of the great women's players from yesterday and today.

Nancy Lieberman

Nancy Lieberman brought the no-look pass to the women's game, and before Magic Johnson ever suited up for the L.A. Lakers, she was known as "Lady Magic." She played collegiate basketball at Old Dominion and led her school to a pair of national championships. Nancy also played two years in the United States Basketball League and played for the Washington Generals, which are the touring opponent for the Harlem Globetrotters. She

TIP-IN

Nancy came back at age 50 in 2008 to play one game for the Detroit Shock, which had received several suspensions the previous game. She contributed two assists in an 18-point loss to Houston and then resumed her job as a TV commentator.

was also the youngest member of the US Women's Olympic team that won a silver medal at the 1976 Olympics. In 1997, though almost forty years old, Nancy played one season for the WNBA's inaugural campaign for the Phoenix Mercury.

Cheryl Miller

Cheryl Miller was a dominant, free-wheeling player for the University of Southern California. She led the team to NCAA titles in 1983 and 1984. She was a leader of the team that won Olympic gold in 1984. A Hall of Famer, Cheryl was widely regarded as the best women's basketball player of all time when she retired. At USC, she set records for points—3,018—and rebounds—1,534. After working as an NBA commentator, Cheryl joined the WNBA as a general manager and coach with the Phoenix Mercury. In 2014, after working as a basketball reporter for TNT, Cheryl became head coach for the women's basketball team at Langston University in central Oklahoma and, more recently, at California State Los Angeles.

Teresa Edwards

Though she came along before the WNBA's glory days, few have accomplished more in women's basketball than Teresa Edwards, who made her name playing professionally overseas. She also has the unprecedented distinction of being the only five-time female US Olympic basketball player. The point guard led the University of Georgia to a pair of Final Four appearances before leading Team USA to four gold medals and one bronze Olympic medal. Teresa played for the fledgling American Basketball League before it folded and was the only ABL player to score more than 40 points in a game. The ABL was a women's professional league that was started in 1996 but folded in 1998 because it didn't have enough money. Teresa is currently assistant coach of the WNBA team the Atlanta Dream based in Atlanta, Georgia.

★ FUN FACTS ★

Cheryl's family had a lot of athletic talent. Her brother Reggie was one of the NBA's great shooters during his career with the Indiana Pacers and another brother, Darrell, was a Major League Baseball catcher for four years with the California Angels.

Rebecca Lobo

One of the best college basketball players of all time, Rebecca Lobo helped Connecticut become a force in women's college basketball. There was no stopping Rebecca; at 6 feet 4 inches, she was very agile and graceful with the ball and was seldom beaten for a rebound. She set her state's high school scoring record with 2,710 points in Massachusetts, and at UConn she became the nation's best player in 1995, leading the Huskies to the national championship and a perfect 35–0 season. That year, Rebecca won Naismith and College Player of the Year awards. Her WNBA career with the New York Liberty started out strong, but a torn knee ligament brought her pro career to a premature end. In 2017, Rebecca was inducted into the Basketball Hall of Fame. She currently works as a TV analyst and motivational speaker.

Pick Up the Pieces

These girls are looking for a game of pick-up, but something has gone wrong. Can you put this back together and see what it is?

Ann Meyers

Ann Meyers was the first woman to sign a contract with an NBA team, getting a three-day tryout with the Indiana Pacers. Though she was cut from the team, the following year Ann was drafted into the Women's Professional Basketball League and played just one season, 1979–1980, in which she was named Most Valuable Player. But her standout performances were as an amateur. As a high school senior in 1974, Ann became the first prep player named to a US basketball team. She followed that up with a spot on the 1976 US Olympic team, which won silver. She was also UCLA's first female full-ride scholarship student athlete. As a Lady Bruin, the 5-foot-9-inch Ann had a quadruple-double—20 points, 14 rebounds, 10 assists, and 10 steals—the only player, male or female, to do that in school history. Ann led UCLA to the 1978 national championship. She is currently vice president of the WNBA team Phoenix Mercury, based in Phoenix, Arizona.

WNBA Stars

The WNBA was founded in 1996 and started play in 1997, building off the momentum of the 1996 Olympics in which the US women's team won the gold medal and gained a lot of attention in the media. Most teams are in cities that also have NBA teams. The exception was the Connecticut Sun, which is located in a state that also has one of the nation's most successful and high-profile college women's programs at the University of Connecticut. The only other team not to have an NBA team in the same city is the Seattle Storm, though that only came about when the Seattle SuperSonics relocated to Oklahoma City.

★ **FUN FACTS** ★

Ann married Hall of Fame baseball pitcher Don Drysdale and had three children with the former Dodgers great. Ann's brother, Dan, also played for UCLA and then for the Milwaukee Bucks. He was drafted by the L.A. Lakers but was one of four players traded to get Kareem Abdul-Jabbar from the Bucks.

Autographs today!
Meet your favorite WNBA Player here!
"Have your jerseys signed too!"

Cynthia Cooper: Houston Comets

Cynthia Cooper is one of the mainstays of the WNBA; she won four WNBA championships as a guard with the Houston Comets. As a player, Cynthia was a scoring machine, with a career average of 21 points per game. She is the league's all-time points-per-game leader. Cynthia had a 92-game streak in which she scored double figures while in the WNBA. She was inducted into the Women's Basketball Hall of Fame in 2009 and was voted one of the top fifteen players in WNBA history in 2011.

CYNTHIA COOPER

Points	Rebounds	Assists
21.0	3.2	4.9

Sheryl Swoopes: Houston Comets, Seattle Storm, Tulsa Shock

Sheryl Swoopes is the first WNBA player to earn league MVP honors three times. Though her 16-points-per-game career scoring average is eye-popping, she's also been the league's most valuable player of the year in 2000, 2002, and 2005 and its defensive player of the year in 2000, 2002, and 2003. Sheryl led the Houston Comets to four WNBA championships, including one in the league's first season. She also has three Olympic gold medals. Sheryl returned to the WNBA at the age of forty to play for the Tulsa Shock. In August of 2011, Sheryl made the final shot in their game against the Los Angeles Sparks to end the Shock's twenty-game losing streak.

SHERYL SWOOPES

Points	Rebounds	Assists
15.0	4.9	3.2

Diana Taurasi: Phoenix Mercury

A career 20-points-per-game scorer in the WNBA, Diana Taurasi showed how complete she is as a player by averaging more than four assists and four rebounds per game as well. As a college player, Diana was the ultimate winner, leading her team to national championships three years in a row—2002, 2003, and 2004. She finished college as the first Big East

DIANA TAURASI

Points	Rebounds	Assists
19.8	4.0	4.3

player with more than 2,000 points, 600 rebounds, and 600 assists. Diana has won three WNBA championships and won the WNBA MVP award in 2009. She has been selected to nine WNBA All-Star Teams and thirteen All-WNBA Teams. In 2017, she became the all-time leading scorer in WNBA history.

Candace Parker: Los Angeles Sparks

In the 2008 season—her rookie year—Candace Parker averaged 19 points a game, almost 10 rebounds, and exactly four assists for the Los Angeles Sparks. She was named the female athlete of the year by the Associated Press that year. Candace was the college player of the year in 2007, when she led Tennessee to a national championship. Though Tennessee has had great college players through the decades, Candace was the fastest one to score 1,000 points, doing that in just her fifty-sixth career game. She accomplished all that in just two years at Tennessee, despite having to redshirt as a freshman because of a pair of knee injuries. She won the WNBA Championship in 2016 and has twice been named WBNA MVP, once in 2008 and once in 2013, She has been named to five All-Star Games and eight All-WNBA Teams.

CANDACE PARKER

Points	Rebounds	Assists
17.5	8.7	3.9

Lisa Leslie: Los Angeles Sparks

Lisa Leslie, who once scored 101 points in the first half of a high school game, won the WNBA MVP award three times. She was a well-balanced force in the front court and back, averaging 17.3 points and 9.1 rebounds per game. Lisa won two WNBA titles and three WNBA MVP awards. Lisa was chosen for eight All-Star Games and twelve All-WNBA Teams over her pro career. In 2015, Lisa was honored for her excellence in WNBA history when she was elected to the Naismith Memorial Basketball Hall of Fame.

LISA LESLIE

Points	Rebounds	Assists
17.3	9.1	2.4

Amazing Athletes

Sometimes you have to have a good eye to spot a good player on the court. Can you find the players on this court?

Sue Bird • Tamika Catchings • Lisa Leslie • Nancy Lieberman •
Cheryl Miller • Sheryl Swoopes • Rebecca Lobo

```
H C H E R Y L M I L L E R E R
K V K E L D I I U N B O P S U
D U I J K X S U E B I R D T E
N V E I D H A L F L D F E Y E
A N A N C Y L I E B E R M A N
O O J S W C E H T A M I L L E
S H E R Y L S W O O P E S M I
C H E C A T L C W O B I R B S
N A N C E L I B O O R N A M L
R E B R E B E C C A L O B O R
T A M I K A C A T C H I N G S
```

I GOT YOU, BABE

One of basketball's first famous players was Babe Didrikson. She played in the 1920s. The Associated Press named her the greatest female athlete of the first half of the twentieth century. In addition to basketball, she excelled in other sports, including golf, swimming, and track and field.

☆ *87* ☆

Tally Ho!

The final score of this game was 72–79. Which groups of numbers add up to those scores?

20 + 40 + 10 + 3 = _____

25 + 25 + 15 + 6 = _____

34 + 10 + 8 + 10 + 10 = _____

11 + 11 + 11 + 11 + 25 = _____

1 + 1 + 60 + 3 + 13 = _____

22 + 22 + 22 + 10 = _____

9 + 9 + 9 + 27 + 26 = _____

16 + 10 + 10 + 10 + 10 + 23 = _____

The WNBA's All-Decade Team

In 2006, the WNBA selected its All-Decade team after the league's tenth year:

WNBA ALL-DECADE TEAM

Name	WNBA Team (Current/Last Team)
Sue Bird	Seattle Storm
Tamika Catchings	Indiana Fever
Cynthia Cooper	Houston Comets
Yolanda Griffith	Sacramento Monarchs
Lauren Jackson	Seattle Storm
Lisa Leslie	Los Angeles Sparks
Katie Smith	New York Liberty/Seattle Storm
Dawn Staley	Houston Comets/Charlotte Sting
Sheryl Swoopes	Tulsa Shock/Seattle Storm
Tina Thompson	Seattle Storm/Los Angeles Sparks

HONORABLE MENTION

Name	WNBA Team (Current/Last Team)
Ruthie Bolton	Sacramento Monarchs
Chamique Holdsclaw	San Antonio Silver Stars/Atlanta Dream
Ticha Penicheiro	Chicago Sky/Los Angeles Sparks
Diana Taurasi	Phoenix Mercury
Teresa Weatherspoon	Los Angeles Sparks/New York Liberty

6

Coaches

TIP-IN

John almost didn't end up at UCLA. He was ready to accept the head coaching job at the University of Minnesota because his wife wanted to stay in the Midwest, but telephone outages due to bad weather prevented Minnesota from offering him the job. John thought they were no longer interested, so he accepted the UCLA position.

John Wooden

John Wooden was a coach through and through. Keeping college basketball in the nation's mindset while the NBA gained popularity, John built the most consistent, successful program in the history of college basketball. At UCLA, he won a record ten national championships and groomed such future NBA greats as Kareem Abdul-Jabbar and Bill Walton. Dubbed the "Wizard of Westwood," the city in which UCLA is located, John was always a dignified man.

John's career college coaching record was 664–162, winning a little more than 80 percent of his games. He coached twenty-seven seasons at UCLA, stepping down in 1975. He won seven national championships in a row—1966–1973—and amassed a record of thirty-eight NCAA tournament wins in a row. John also set the men's regular-season wins-in-a-row record with eighty-eight. He is also the only coach to guide four undefeated teams (all four went 31–0), and he was the first person to be inducted into the Hall of Fame as both a player and coach.

As a player, John captained Purdue for two successful years as a guard, winning a pair of Big Ten titles and the 1932 national championship. Before beginning his college coaching career, John taught English at South Bend Central High School, near the Notre Dame campus, and coached the high school to a record of 218–42. His incredible journey then took him into the military, as an officer in the Navy for three years during World War II. After the war, he served as athletic director, coach, and teacher at Indiana Teachers College, later renamed Indiana State University—the college where Larry Bird would eventually star.

Follow the Rules!

If you want your team to win, it helps to have a great coach. This coach is very tough. Can you see how these players can get through the obstacle course?

THIS COACH
HAS WHEELS

Why was Cinderella such a bad basketball player?

Her coach was a pumpkin!

Arnold "Red" Auerbach

When Arnold "Red" Auerbach passed away in late 2006 at age 89, the NBA lost a legend, but he left a lot of memories behind. Red actually started with the Washington Capitols and the Tri-Cities Hawks before joining Boston in 1950, where he would be part of the franchise for the next fifty-six years. He got off to the right start in Boston, trading two players to St. Louis for the right to draft Bill Russell, the cornerstone Red built an NBA dynasty around. He coached the Celtics to nine championships, including eight in a row. Even though he could have added more titles to his coaching resume, Red stepped back into the general manager role, acquiring key players to engineer an additional pair of titles in 1968 and 1969.

The Celtics struggled in the 1970s, but when Red saw Larry Bird, he saw the future of his franchise. Getting Bird in the coop was solid, but Red knew he needed to get several more players to complement Bird's skill. He drew the first and thirteenth picks of the 1981 draft to get center Robert Parish and a draft pick, which he used to draft Kevin McHale. He rescued Dennis Johnson and Bill Walton from their careers in the Northwest and revived them, fitting them into the mix to make the Celtics a smart, deep team. The addition of heady guard Danny Ainge, who annoyed opponents to the point of fits, was sheer brilliance.

Pat Summitt

When someone says "the best coach in history," there is usually room for debate. When it comes to women's basketball, there is no debate, because no one has ever equaled the success of Pat Summitt. The University of Tennessee Hall of Fame coach just kept putting winners on the court year after year. After repeating an NCAA championship in 2008—for her eighth NCAA title at Tennessee—Pat remains the coach with the most wins in college history, women's or men's. During her career, she went 1,098–208, winning 84.1 percent of her games. Under Pat, Tennessee made a record sixteen consecutive Final Fours in a row and a record 27

Everybody Chant

Words have a lot of power to motivate us. This player has decided to write a song for her team. It looks like she's having trouble with the final word in each line. Can you help her out? (Hint: the last words all rhyme.)

The game is on, it's getting l___ ___ ___

The score's close, 87 to 8 ___

It's up to you to decide their f___ ___ ___!

Make us proud of our s ___ ___ ___ ___;

Let's tell the players we think they're g ___ ___ ___ ___!

A coach was having trouble with one of his players, so he took him aside for a talk. "What's the problem? Is it ignorance or apathy?" The player replied, "I don't know and I don't care!"

appearances in the Sweet 16. She has produced twelve Olympic players, and every single one of her players who completed their eligibility at Tennessee graduated with their degrees. Pat retired from coaching in 2012, the same year she was awarded the Presidential Medal of Freedom by President Obama and the ESPY Awards granted her the Arthur Ashe Courage Award. Pat has coauthored three books with Sally Jenkins; the third book, *Sum It Up*, published by Three Rivers Press in 2014, includes Pat's diagnosis of early-onset Alzheimer's disease.

Pat Riley

With his slicked-back hair, Pat Riley was the conductor of the Lakers' "Showtime" production that included Magic Johnson, James Worthy, Kareem Abdul-Jabbar, and three NBA titles. Pat left to coach the New York Knicks, where he showed he could coach a physical style of play. Despite taking New York to the Finals, he could not win an NBA championship. Coaxed to Florida to get the expansion Miami Heat up to the elite NBA standards, Pat built a solid group of veterans around young superstar Dwyane Wade. Once Pat was able to land Shaquille O'Neal from the Lakers, the Heat turned up the temperature on the rest of the league and brought Miami its first NBA Championship.

Mike "Coach K" Krzyzewski

Considering where his playing and coaching roots were planted, it's no surprise that Mike Krzyzewski's teams are disciplined and fundamentally sound. Mike played and coached at the US Military Academy at West Point. He left the Army for Duke in 1980, and thus began a dominating coaching performance for the ages. Under Mike, Duke has won five national championships, and he has more than 1,100 coaching wins, the most of any head coach in basketball history. He has been Naismith College Coach of the Year three times. Mike coached the United States Olympic team in 2008 in Beijing, in 2012 in London, and in 2016 in Rio.

Dean Smith

When he retired, North Carolina's Dean Smith had the most wins in college basketball history. But for the Tar Heels, Dean was more than a coach—he was an institution. In thirty-six years as head coach, he won 879 games and had just 254 losses. Dean's Tar Heels won national championships in 1982 and 1993, and 96 percent of his student athletes graduated. Dean also coached the US Olympic team to the gold medal in 1976.

Bobby Knight

Bobby Knight won a pair of national championships at the University of Indiana and when he retired, he led all men's college basketball coaches with 902 career victories. His teams, with a few exceptions, did not have superstars who turned into NBA greats, but they played good defense and had solid fundamentals—and they never stopped hustling. Bobby also coached the US Olympic basketball team to a gold medal in 1984. After coaching at Indiana, he moved on to coach in the Big 12 at Texas Tech University before stepping aside. Bobby was succeeded at Tech by his son, longtime assistant coach Pat Knight.

Don Haskins

Don Haskins set the bar high, winning 719 games as a head coach, including the national championship with Texas Western in 1966. At the time Don coached, not all coaches were giving black players a chance to play. Don was the first Division I coach to start five black

Crazy Coach

Coaches often use code so the other team can't understand their next play. But this coach looks like he's just being silly. Can you figure out the first letter of these silly sayings?

___un ___ound
___obin ___egularly

___on't ___ribble ___owntown

___erfect ___layers ___lay ___olitely

___onight ___all ___eams
___ake ___urns

___rateful ___uards
___et ___oals

players, and his team beat a heavily favored University of Kentucky team for the national championship. In his thirty-eight-year career, Don took his team to fourteen NCAA tournaments.

Adolph Rupp

Adolph Rupp's success in winning games and championships for the University of Kentucky are part of college basketball's history. His Wildcats claimed four national championships in the 1940s and 1950s. Adolph built a program at Kentucky that to this day is seen as one of the premier programs in the country and has drawn talented coaches such as Rick Pitino to Lexington. Adolph was a backup player for legendary Kansas coach Phog Allen, who was assisted by the very founder of basketball, James Naismith.

Phil Jackson

As coach of the Chicago Bulls, Phil Jackson had the best player in the world in Michael Jordan. Phil's six titles with the Chicago Bulls were a run not seen in decades. He added three more championship wins with Kobe Bryant, Shaquille O'Neal, and the Lakers. In 2009 and 2010, he won his tenth and eleventh NBA championships with Kobe and the Lakers, passing coaching great Red Auerbach for most titles ever. Phil was named President of the New York Knickerbockers (Knicks) on March 18, 2014, before leaving the Knicks in 2017.

7

Hall of Fame

Finding a Home for the Hall

The Naismith Memorial Basketball Hall of Fame is in Springfield, Massachusetts, and enshrines not just players and coaches but referees and other major contributors to the game. It also includes eight entire teams. The Hall is dedicated to preserving basketball history and is considered the greatest historical asset of the game. It was established in 1959, though an actual facility did not open until 1968 at Springfield College, where James Naismith started the sport with peach baskets as an effort to build teamwork and keep his students physically active during cold winter months.

In 2002, the Hall of Fame opened its current 40,000-square-foot building. As they approach, fans are greeted by the sight of a huge silver basketball and an orange globe atop sky-reaching spires.

The Hall has three floors. The Honors Ring overlooks the entire Hall. It has photos and a display of Hall of Famers' artifacts including shoes, jerseys, and basketballs. The second floor has the Players Gallery, the Hooperactive Zone, Coaches Gallery, Broadcast section, and College section, which has most of the items in the Hall. There are also exhibits that show how the game was invented, including handwritten notes and speeches from Naismith. The Hall's Center Court features a full basketball court where fans can shoot baskets.

Induction

The Naismith Hall of Fame is unique because it includes international professionals and both US and international amateurs. The Hall has four separate screening committees for American candidates, female candidates, international candidates, and veteran candidates. Veteran candidates must have been retired at least thirty-five years before being nominated.

To be eligible for the Hall of Fame, players must be retired for at least five years. Referees must either be retired for five years or have at least twenty-five years as a referee at the high school, college, amateur, or professional level. No specific criteria exist for contributor inductees, but the person must have made a "significant contribution" to the game of basketball, and has included several famous broadcasters and sports writers. Contributors who have been inducted into the Hall of Fame include broadcasters like Dick Vitale, who has been an analyst with ESPN for more than thirty years.

The Naismith Hall also decides and presents several awards to collegiate players each year. The Bob Cousy Award has been presented since 2004 to the top point guard selected from Divisions I, II, and III. The Frances Pomeroy Naismith Award is presented to the female player less than 68 inches in height and male player less than 72 inches in height determined to have been that year's top student athlete. The men's award is voted on by the National Association of Basketball Coaches; the women's award is voted on by the Women's Basketball Coaches Association.

WORDS TO KNOW

Honors Committee
An Honors Committee of 12 permanent members and a rotating 12-member committee made up of specialists vote on candidates. Anyone who receives 18 votes, or 75 percent, from the Honors Committee is approved for enshrinement in the Hall of Fame. The committee can decide not to consider a potential nominee who has damaged the integrity of basketball.

HALL OF FAME PLAYERS

Kareem Abdul-Jabbar, 1995	Zelmo Beaty, 2016	William W. Bradley, 1982	Charles "Chuck" Cooper, 2019
Ray Allen, 2018	John Beckman, 1972	Carl Braun, 2019	
Nathaniel Archibald, 1991	Walter Bellamy, 1993	Joseph R. Brennan, 1974	Charles T. Cooper, 1976
Paul J. Arizin, 1977	Sergei Belov, 1992	Roger Brown, 2013	Cynthia Cooper-Dyke, 2010
Charles Barkley, 2006	David Bing, 1990	Alfred N. Cervi, 1984	Kresimir Cosic, 1996
Thomas B. Barlow, 1980	Larry Bird, 1998	Wilton N. Chamberlain, 1978	Robert J. Cousy, 1970
Richard F. Barry, 1987	Carol Blazejowski, 1994	Maurice Cheeks, 2018	David W. Cowens, 1991
Elgin Baylor, 1976	Bernard Borgmann, 1961	Zack Clayton, 2017	Joan Crawford, 1997

William J. Cunningham, 1986
Denise Curry, 1997
Drazen Dalipagic, 2004
Louie Dampier, 2015
Mel Daniels, 2012
Adrian Dantly, 2008
Robert E. Davies, 1969
Forrest S. DeBernardi, 1961
David A. DeBusschere, 1982
Henry G. Dehnert, 1968
Vlade Divac, 2019
Anne Donovan, 1995
Clyde Drexler, 2004
Joe Dumars, 2006
Teresa Edwards, 2011
Paul Endacott, 1971
Alex English, 1997
Julius W. Erving, 1993
Patrick Ewing, 2008
Harold E. Foster, 1964
Walter Frazier, 1987
Max Friedman, 1971
Joseph F. Fulks, 1977
Lauren Gale, 1976
Nikos Galis, 2017
Harry J. Gallatin, 1991
William "Pop" Gates, 1989
George Gervin, 1996
Artis Gilmore, 2011
Thomas J. Gola, 1975
Gail Goodrich, 1996
Harold E. Greer, 1981
Robert F. Gruenig, 1963
Richie Guerin, 2013
Clifford O. Hagan, 1977
Victor A. Hanson, 1960
Lusia Harris-Stewart, 1992
John Havlicek, 1983

Cornelius L. Hawkins, 1992
Elvin E. Hayes, 1990
Marques Haynes, 1998
Spencer Haywood, 2015
Thomas W. Heinsohn, 1986
Grant Hill, 2018
Nat Holman, 1964
Robert J. Houbregs, 1987
Bailey Howell, 1997
Charles D. Hyatt, 1959
John Isaacs, 2015
Daniel P. Issel, 1993
Allen Iverson, 2016
Harry "Buddy" Jeannette, 1994
Dennis Johnson, 2010
Earvin "Magic" Johnson Jr., 2002
Gus Johnson, 2010
William C. Johnson, 1976
Donald Neil Johnston, 1990
Bobby Jones, 2019
K.C. Jones, 1989
Samuel "Sam" Jones, 1983
Michael Jordan, 2009
Jason Kidd, 2018
Bernard King, 2013
Edward W. Krause, 1975
Robert A. Kurland, 1961
Robert J. Lanier, 1992
Joe Lapchick, 1966
Lisa Leslie, 2015
Nancy Lieberman, 1996
Rebecca Lobo, 2017
Clyde E. Lovellette, 1988
Jerry R. Lucas, 1979
Angelo Luisetti, 1959
Hortencia Marcari, 2005
Branch McCracken, 1960
Edward C. Macauley, 1960

Ubiratan Pereira Maciel, 2010
Karl Malone, 2010
Moses Malone, 2001
Peter P. Maravich, 1987
Sarunas Marciulionis, 2014
Slater N. Martin, 1981
Robert McAdoo, 2000
Katrina McClain, 2012
Jack McCracken, 1962
Robert McDermott, 1988
George McGinnis, 2017
Richard S. McGuire, 1993
Tracy McGrady, 2017
Kevin McHale, 1999
Dino Meneghin, 2003
Ann E. Meyers, 1993
George L. Mikan, 1959
Vern Mikkelsen, 1995
Cheryl Miller, 1995
Reggie Miller, 2012
Yao Ming, 2016
Sidney Moncrief, 2019
Vernon Earl Monroe, 1990
Alonzo Mourning, 2014
Chris Mullen, 2011
Calvin J. Murphy, 1993
Charles C. Murphy, 1960
Dikembe Mutombo, 2015
Steve Nash, 2018
Hakeem Olajuwon, 2008
Shaquille O'Neal, 2016
Harlan O. Page, 1962
Robert Parish, 2003
Gary Payton, 2013
Drazen Petrovic, 2002
Robert L. Pettit, 1970
Andy Phillip, 1961
Scottie Pippen, 2010

James C. Pollard, 1977
Cumberland Posey, 2016
Dino Radja, 2018
Frank V. Ramsey, 1981
Willis Reed Jr., 1981
Mitch Richmond, 2014
Arnold "Arnie" Risen, 1998
Oscar P. Robertson, 1979
David Robinson, 2009
Guy Rodgers, 2014
Dennis Rodman, 2011
John S. Roosma, 1961
John D. Russell, 1964
William F. Russell, 1974
Arvydas Sabonis, 2011
Ralph Sampson, 2012
Adolph Schayes, 1972
Ernest J. Schmidt, 1973
Oscar Schmidt, 2013
John J. Schommer, 1959
Charlie Scott, 2018
Barney Sedran, 1962
Uljana Semjonova, 1993
Bill W. Sharman, 1975
Jack Sikma, 2019
Katie Smith, 2018
Dawn Staley, 2013
Christian Steinmetz, 1961
John Stockton, 2009
Maurice Stokes, 2004
Sheryl Swoopes, 2016
Isiah Thomas, 2000
David Thompson, 1996
John A. Thompson, 1962
Tina Thompson, 2018
Nate Thurmond, 1984
John "Jack" K. Twyman, 1982
Westley S. Unseld, 1988

HALL OF FAME

Robert P. Vandivier, 1974
Edward A. Wachter, 1961
Chet Walker, 2012
William T. Walton, 1993
Robert Wanzer, 1987
Ora Mae Washington, 2018

Teresa Weatherspoon, 2019
Jerry A. West, 1979
Paul Westphal, 2019
Joseph Henry "Jo Jo" White, 2015
Nera D. White, 1992

Leonard "Lenny" Wilkens, 1989
Jamaal Wilkes, 2012
Dominique Wilkins, 2006
Lynette Woodard, 2004
John R. Wooden, 1960

James Worthy, 2003
George Yardley, 1996

HALL OF FAME COACHES

Lidia Alexeeva, 2012
Forrest Clare Allen, 1959
W. Harold Anderson, 1984
Arnold "Red" Auerbach, 1968
Geno Auriemma, 2006
Leon Barmore, 2003
Justin M. "Sam" Barry, 1978
Ernest A. Blood, 1960
Jim Boeheim, 2005
Larry Brown, 2002
Jim Calhoun, 2005
John Calipari, 2015
Howard G. Cann, 1967
Henry Clifford Carlson, 1959
Louis P. Carnesecca, 1992
Bernard L. Carnevale, 1969
Pete Carril, 1997
Everett N. Case, 1981
Van Chancellor, 2007
John Chaney, 2001
Jody Conradt, 1998
Denzil "Denny" E. Crum, 1994
Charles J. Daly, 1994
Everett S. Dean, 1966
Antonio Diaz-Miguel, 1997
Edgar A. Diddle, 1971
Bruce Drake, 1972
Charles Driesel, 2018

Pedro Ferrandiz, 2007
Bill Fitch, 2019
Sandro Gamba, 2006
Clarence E. Gaines, 1981
James H. "Jack" Gardner, 1983
Lindsay Gaze, 2015
Amory T. Gill, 1967
Aleksandr Gomelsky, 1995
Sue Gunter, 2005
Alexander "Alex" Hannum, 1998
Marv K. Harshman, 1984
Don Haskins, 1997
Sylvia Hatchell, 2013
Tommy Heinsohn, 2015
Edgar S. Hickey, 1978
Howard A. Hobson, 1965
William "Red" Holzman, 1986
Robert Hughes, 2017
Bob Hurley, 2010
Henry P. Iba, 1968
Tom Izzo, 2016
Phil Jackson, 2007
Alvin F. Julian, 1967
Frank W. Keaney, 1960
George E. Keogan, 1961
Robert M. Knight, 1991

Mike Krzyzewski, 2001
John Kundla, 1995
Ward L. Lambert, 1960
Bobby Leonard, 2014
Guy Lewis, 2013
Harry Litwack, 1975
Kenneth D. Loeffler, 1964
Arthur C. Lonborg, 1972
Herb Magee, 2011
Arad A. McCutchan, 1980
Alfred J. McGuire, 1992
Frank J. McGuire, 1976
Muffet McGraw, 2017
John McLendon, 2016
Walter E. Meanwell, 1959
Raymond J. Meyer, 1978
Ralph H. Miller, 1988
Billie Moore, 1999
Don Nelson, 2012
Aleksandar Nikolic, 1998
Mirko Novosel, 2007
Lute Olson, 2002
Rick Pitino, 2013
John "Jack" T. Ramsay, 1992
Pat Riley, 2008
Nolan Richardson, 2014
Cesare Rubini, 1994
Adolph F. Rupp, 1968

Cathy Rush, 2008
Leonard D. Sachs, 1961
Bill Self, 2017
Bill W. Sharman, 2004
Everett F. Shelton, 1979
Jerry Sloan, 2009
Dean E. Smith, 1982
Charlaine Vivian Stringer, 2009
Pat Head Summitt, 2000
Jerry Tarkanian, 2013
Fred R. Taylor, 1986
John Thompson, 1999
Tara VanDerveer, 2011
L. Margaret Wade, 1984
Stanley H. Watts, 1986
Leonard "Lenny" Wilkens, 1998
Gary Williams, 2014
Roy Williams, 2007
John R. Wooden, 1972
Phil Woolpert, 1992
Morgan Wootten, 2000
Kay Yow, 2002

Lost in a Crowd

When you're a famous sports figure, everybody knows what you do. Look at this crowd of people and see if you can pick out the famous players. They have 1 stripe on their shorts, a headband, and 2 long socks.

Most places around the world use the same word for basketball as we do, but some languages have their own word. In Italian it's *basket*. In Polish it's *koszykówka*. In Portuguese it's *basquete*, and in Spanish it's *baloncesto*.

HALL OF FAME TEAMS

Buffalo Germans, 1961

Original Celtics, 1959

The First Team, 1959

New York Rens, 1963

The Harlem Globetrotters, 2002

Texas Western, 2007

All-American Red Heads, 2012

Immaculata College, 2014

1960 US Olympic team, 2010

1992 US Olympic team, 2010

Tennessee A&I, 2019

Wayland Baptist University, 2019

The teams in the Hall of Fame include James Naismith's first team of 18 players who were studying at Springfield when James came up with the game of basketball. The team was inducted in 1959 at the inaugural induction and opening of the Hall of Fame. The Buffalo Germans were formed in 1895 at the Buffalo Eastside YMCA. In 1904, they won the National AAU Tournament, which served as an exhibition sport at the St. Louis Olympics.

An all-black team, the New York Renaissance, known also as the Rens, is also in the Hall. It was formed in 1923 by Robert Douglas. Though the team played home games at the Harlem Renaissance Casino and Ballroom, it became famous for barnstorming the nation, playing teams nationally. The team had a record of 112–8, winning eighty-eight games in a row at one point. It was the first black team to win a national tournament, beating the National Basketball League's Oshkosh All-Stars. The Rens had a career record of 2,588–539 and disbanded in 1949.

Another great barnstorming team in the Hall of Fame is the Original Celtics (no relation to the Boston Celtics), which was a pro touring team in the 1920s. The team was an offshoot of the New York Celtics, with several players from that team and added players mostly from New York City's West Side. The team played in several fledgling leagues before deciding to tour nationwide, playing about 175 games a year. The team

★ FUN FACTS ★

From 1908 to 1911, the Germans won 111 games, which was an incredible total of victories, especially considering how new the sport was.

WORDS TO KNOW

Barnstorming
This means to travel around the country playing in small and big towns, wherever a game can be set up.

Double Duty

This Hall of Fame is very unique . . . or maybe not. There are two of them! Can you spot the 7 differences?

won 90 percent of its games, and its 1922–1923 record of 193–11–1 is still among the most awe-inspiring in basketball history. The team was forced to join the American Basketball League in 1926 because teams would not otherwise play the Celtics. The Celtics dominated the league so much in the first two seasons that the league disbanded the team and farmed out its players to other teams.

The Harlem Globetrotters, an entertainment act with basketball skill and verve, is another Hall of Fame team. It was formed in 1926 and has played more than 26,000 games in 123 countries. The team's beginnings are disputed, but it is a favorite of fans worldwide, with amazing dribblers, crazy shots that always seem to go in, and a playfulness that delights spectators around the world. They also have a lot of talent. Early on, they beat the George Mikan–led Minneapolis Lakers in 1948 and 1949.

The 1966 Texas Western team (now the University of Texas at El Paso) made history when coach Don Haskins became the first to start five black players in college basketball. Texas Western beat Adolph Rupp's powerhouse University of Kentucky in the national championship game, 72–65. The 2006 movie *Glory Road* is based on the 1966 Texas Western season.

8

The NBA Finals

The Champions by Year

People remember players, but players remember league championships—in this case, the NBA Finals. You have heard someone ask, "But how many rings did that player have?" Fair or not, championships are the stick by which most of the great players are measured. Here's a brief rundown of the NBA Finals through the years. To get to the Finals, teams go through a series of playoff games. Eight teams in the Western Conference and eight teams in the Eastern Conference battle each other to get to the Finals. Teams play in a best-of-seven series; the first team in a series to win four games advances to the next round, and the loser is out of the playoffs. Eventually, there are only two teams left—one from each conference. These two teams play each other for the NBA championship.

1947   The Basketball Association of America's first league championship involved two of America's most famous cities, Chicago and Philadelphia. The Philadelphia Warriors of the Eastern Conference were led by future Hall of Famer Joe Fulks. They downed the Western Conference's Chicago Stags in five games, and Philadelphia claimed the league's first title.

1948   In a blow to Philadelphia's dominance, the Baltimore Bullets needed only six games to down the Warriors to win Baltimore's first league championship in a 4–2 series.

1949   Minneapolis Lakers center George Mikan became one of the league's first outstanding big men. George Mikan, 6 feet 10 inches, led his team past the Washington Capitols in a series that went six games, 4–2.

1950   In the 1950 Finals, Minneapolis became the first repeat winner, downing the Syracuse Nationals, again in a six-game series, 4–2.

1951 The Rochester Royals and New York Knicks turned the basketball nation's eyes on the state of New York as Rochester won in a series that went the full seven games, 4–3.

1952 Two years after their repeat championship, the Minneapolis Lakers came back and made it count, beating the Knicks—who lost in the Finals for the second year in a row—in another exciting seven-game series.

1953 The Minneapolis Lakers and Knicks had a repeat of the previous year's Finals, and while the champion was the same—the Lakers—the series only went five games; the Knicks won just once.

1954 For the fifth time in the league's eight-year history, the Minneapolis Lakers claimed the league championships, surviving the Syracuse Nationals, four games to three.

★ FUN FACTS ★

The Rochester Royals are still around today, although they're not known by that name. The franchise has moved all over the country, playing in Cincinnati and Kansas City before becoming the Sacramento Kings in 1985. Their 1951 title is still their only one.

1955 After going to the league Finals twice and losing, Syracuse finally got it together and claimed its first championship by defeating the Fort Wayne Pistons in seven games.

1956 Fort Wayne made it back to the Finals, but the Pistons once again came up a little short. The Philadelphia Warriors claimed their first title since winning the inaugural championship, easily beating the Pistons 4–1.

1957 This was the start of something special for Boston. The Celtics made their first time to the Finals count, beating the St. Louis Hawks in a series that went the full seven games.

1958 In a feel-good story that would last only one year, the St. Louis Hawks returned to the Finals and beat the Boston Celtics in six games.

1959 The Celtics were back on track and rolled to their second title in three years, recording the Finals first 4–0 sweep by beating the five-time league champion Minnesota Lakers.

1960 The Boston Celtics took on the St. Louis Hawks once again, and they needed all seven games to win their third title in four years. The league's first true dynasty had kicked into high gear.

1961 Though the proud St. Louis Hawks made it back to the Finals, they were but a speed bump for Boston, beating the Celtics only

Tag Team

In basketball, each player has to be top notch, but it's even more important to be a team player. Can you match each team with its correct city?

Houston	Raptors
Oklahoma City	Heat
Atlanta	Pistons
Los Angeles	Knicks
Toronto	Thunder
New York	Bulls
Boston	Hawks
Detroit	Lakers
Orlando	Magic
Chicago	Celtics
Miami	Rockets

What's the difference between a dog and a basketball player?

One drools and the other dribbles!

once in a series that went five games as the Celtics made it three in a row.

1962 In a preview of what fans would see decades down the road, the Boston Celtics took on the Los Angeles Lakers, and Boston came away with its fourth title in a row and its fifth in six years. But it wasn't easy—the series went the full seven games.

1963 Boston and more Boston. The Celtics needed six games to dispatch the Los Angeles Lakers and win their sixth overall title and fifth in a row.

1964 This time another California team, the San Francisco Warriors, battled the Celtics, but the result was a 4–1 series win for the Boston Celtics.

1965 The Los Angeles Lakers squared off against their familiar nemesis, the Boston Celtics. The Celtics needed just five games to claim their seventh title in a row.

1966 The Los Angeles Lakers put up a fight against the Boston Celtics and pushed the series to seven games. But in the end, the Celtics snagged their eighth title in a row.

1967 The Philadelphia 76ers eliminated the Celtics in the division finals, four games to one. They needed six games to beat the San Francisco Warriors in the Finals, 4–2.

1968 The Celtics faced the familiar Los Angeles Lakers and Los Angeles fell in six games to the Celtics.

1969 The Boston Celtics got more than they imagined from L.A.'s Finals Most Valuable Player Jerry West—the first year the MVP was chosen—but the Lakers were not good enough to overcome the Celtics, as Boston won the league championship 4–3.

1970 After losing in the Finals three times, the New York Knicks finally claimed their first league championship. Willis Reed won the Most Valuable Player award as he led the Knicks in a seven-game victory over Los Angeles.

1971 A 7-foot-3-inch Kareem Abdul-Jabbar put the Milwaukee Bucks into their first NBA Finals. He was named the MVP of the series in a 4–0 sweep of the Baltimore Bullets.

1972 Wilt Chamberlain powered his Los Angeles Lakers to a 4–1 Finals win over the New York Knicks.

1973 Led once again by Finals MVP Willis Reed, the New York Knicks were too much for the L.A. Lakers and emerged victorious in five games.

1974 With a balanced cast of fundamentally deft players, the Boston Celtics and their tenacious defense, led by MVP John Havlicek, downed the Milwaukee Bucks in an exhaustive seven-game series.

1975   The Golden State Warriors brought Northern California and the Bay Area its first NBA Championship, as MVP Rick Barry led the Warriors to a sweep of the Washington Bullets.

1976   For the second time in three years, the Boston Celtics, on the cusp of rebuilding as a franchise, squeezed out another NBA championship. Jo Jo White claimed MVP honors during the Celtics 4–2 rolling of the Phoenix Suns.

1977   Claiming their first—and so far, only—NBA championship, the Portland Trail Blazers made the Pacific Northwest proud. The Blazers got the best out of Bill Walton and beat the Philadelphia 76ers in six games to claim the crown.

1978   The Washington Bullets, led by MVP center Wes Unseld, finally claimed an NBA championship by halting the upstart Seattle SuperSonics in a series that went the entire seven games.

1979   For the second time in three years, fans in the Pacific Northwest had reason to smile, as the Seattle SuperSonics claimed their first NBA championship. Led by MVP Dennis Johnson, the Sonics defeated the Washington Bullets 4–1.

1980   Magic Johnson, the MVP, keyed his Los Angeles Lakers to a 4–2 championship over the Philadelphia 76ers.

1981   The Boston Celtics reclaimed their spot atop the heap with an NBA championship. Cedric Maxwell won the MVP award by leading Boston past the Houston Rockets in a six-game final.

1982   Magic Johnson and the Los Angeles Lakers won their second title in three years by upending the Philadelphia 76ers, once again in six games.

1983   Making it to the NBA Finals for the fourth time in seven years, the Philadelphia 76ers won their first NBA title since 1967, sweeping the Los Angeles Lakers 4–0. Moses Malone earned MVP honors.

1984   Larry Bird was named MVP as he led the Boston Celtics to an exciting seven-game win over the Los Angeles Lakers. It was only a preview of series matchups to come.

1985   Kareem Abdul-Jabbar was the cog that moved the Los Angeles Lakers machine to an NBA championship, some fourteen years after winning his first MVP award—no one else has ever had such a gap between MVP honors. The Lakers downed the rival Boston Celtics in six games.

FUN FACTS

Kareem played in the NBA until age 42, an incredibly advanced age for an NBA player. He credits his long career to staying in shape and eating right, and he practiced meditation as well.

1986   The Celtics made their third trip to the Finals in three years. Behind Bird's second MVP performance, they downed the Houston Rockets in six games.

1987   This was the last of the great Celtics-Lakers matchups for twenty-one years. Magic Johnson won his third MVP award as the Los Angeles Lakers beat the Celtics 4–2.

1988   Los Angeles Lakers power forward James Worthy stepped up for an MVP, boosting Los Angeles past the Detroit Pistons in seven games.

1989   Though the Lakers made it back to the Finals for the eighth time in 10 seasons, the Detroit Pistons were ready for them. Hot-shooting guard Joe Dumars earned MVP honors and sparked the Pistons to a sweep of the aging Lakers.

1990   The Detroit Pistons hit their third NBA Finals in three years. Isiah Thomas earned MVP honors and boosted the Pistons over the Portland Trail Blazers in five games.

1991   Hello, Mr. Jordan. The Chicago Bulls officially became a force in the NBA, ending Detroit's dominance of the Eastern Conference. Michael claimed MVP honors by leading his team past the Los Angeles Lakers in five games, in a series that saw the Lakers make their last Finals appearance until 2000.

1992   The Bulls and Michael, again the MVP, dumped the Portland Trail Blazers in six games for Chicago's second title in a row.

1993   The Bulls returned for their three-peat championship. Michael earned the MVP award for the third time in the Bulls' defeat of the Phoenix Suns.

1994   No Bulls? Not with Michael playing minor league baseball. The scrappy New York Knicks made the Finals, but the Houston Rockets won the tough seven-game series 4–3. The Rockets' Hakeem Olajuwon claimed MVP honors.

1995   The world was introduced to the Orlando Magic's Shaquille O'Neal. But the veteran Houston Rockets swept the Magic in four games and took home the title. Hakeem was MVP.

1996   Michael rejoined Chicago late in the 1994–1995 season and led them back to the playoffs the next season. The Bulls beat the Seattle SuperSonics in six games, with Michael winning his fourth MVP award.

1997   Repeat alert: The Bulls, led by the one and only Michael, won a six-game series to down the Utah Jazz. "His Airness" earned another MVP.

1998   In a mirror image of the previous year's campaign, Michael was MVP as the Bulls beat the Utah Jazz for Chicago's second three-peat in eight years. It was Michael's sixth NBA championship and sixth MVP award.

1999   Young Tim Duncan gave San Antonio the strong, big man to complement David Robinson. That was all the San Antonio Spurs needed to beat the New York Knicks in six games, with Tim earning MVP honors.

2000   The Lakers went from Magic and Kareem to Kobe and Shaquille, with Shaq claiming the MVP award in a six-game championship over the Indiana Pacers.

2001   The Philadelphia 76ers and Allen Iverson could not slow Shaq and his Lakers, who won in just five games. Shaq claimed MVP honors in the Lakers' second title in as many years.

2002   Good things come in threes, and for the third time since Michael won a pair of three-peats, Shaq led the Lakers past their third Finals opponent. The Lakers won in a clean sweep over the New Jersey Nets. Shaq once again earned the MVP award.

2003   The Lakers' domination of the West came to an end as the San Antonio Spurs rose to the challenge. The Spurs cut down the New Jersey Nets in six games in New Jersey's second consecutive trip to the Finals. Tim Duncan won his second MVP honor.

2004   In an Eastern team reminiscent of John Havlicek's balanced Celtics, the Detroit Pistons brought a balanced offense, keyed by MVP Chauncey Billups, to take down the Lakers in a quick five-game final.

2005   San Antonio got another MVP performance from Tim and survived a seven-game series with the defending champion Detroit Pistons.

★ **FUN FACTS** ★

Hakeem never even played basketball until he was seventeen years old, yet he emerged as one of the most dominating centers in NBA history. Though he was—and remains—listed as 7 feet tall on all rosters and stat books, he admits he is barely taller than 6 feet 10 inches.

2006   The Miami Heat signed Shaq for one reason: to win an NBA championship. Dwyane Wade, the MVP, was the guard who ran the show and did most of the scoring as the Heat knocked off Dallas in six games.

2007   The San Antonio Spurs beat LeBron James and the Cleveland Cavaliers in a 4–0 sweep for San Antonio's third NBA crown in five years. Tony Parker nabbed MVP honors.

2008   The Celtics made a big push in the off-season, signing perennial All-Star Kevin Garnett away from Minnesota and getting hot-shooting Ray Allen to team with Paul Pierce. Boston was just too much for the Lakers, winning in six games as Paul earned MVP honors.

★ FUN FACTS ★

Michael's jump shot from the top of the key in the last game of the 1998 Finals is a moment frozen in time for many fans. Michael retired after the win over Utah. Although he returned three years later with the Washington Wizards, he spent the height of his career with the Bulls.

2009   The Los Angeles Lakers beat the Orlando Magic in five games. Kobe Bryant snagged the MVP award, but solid support from teammates Pau Gasol and Trevor Ariza sealed the championship. Lakers coach Phil Jackson earned his tenth championship ring, an all-time NBA record.

2010   Once again, the Los Angeles Lakers went to the championship and this time beat the Boston Celtics in seven games. This was the first NBA Finals to go the full seven games since 2005. Kobe Bryant was awarded the Most Valuable Player award for his second consecutive title.

2011   For the first time in history, the Dallas Mavericks won an NBA title by beating the Miami Heat in six games. Going into the series, the Heat were the heavy favorites with newly acquired LeBron James and Chris Bosh playing alongside Dwyane Wade. Dirk Nowitzki went on to win the Finals MVP, becoming the first German to win the award.

2012   The Miami Heat returned to the NBA Finals to defeat the Oklahoma City Thunder in just five games under coach Erik Spoelstra. LeBron James was awarded the Finals MVP, and the Heat proved they were indeed a powerful force.

2013   The Miami Heat beat the San Antonio Spurs in seven games, bringing home another championship, and becoming the sixth team in history to win consecutive NBA championships. The series also marked the fifth time the

The Detroit Shock captured their first WNBA title in 2003, so the Shock and the Pistons were the reigning champions of their leagues at the same time. It was the first time one city had both NBA and WNBA champions.

Spurs made the NBA Finals since 1999. Once again, LeBron James was awarded the Finals Most Valuable Player.

2014   In a rematch from the championship the year prior, the San Antonio Spurs (under Coach Gregg Popovich) defeated the Miami Heat in five games. The Spurs outscored the Heat in the series by the largest average point differential (14 points) in Finals history. Kawhi Leonard was award the Finals MVP, becoming the third-youngest recipient of the award.

2015   The Golden State Warriors, led by regular season MVP Steph Curry, won an NBA title for the first time in four decades by beating the Cleveland Cavaliers in six games. Despite a dominant performance throughout the series by LeBron James, the Warriors used their smaller, quicker players and strong defense from Finals MVP Andre Iguodala to get their ring.

2016   Another rematch from the previous year, but this time LeBron James and the Cleveland Cavaliers won. Despite being down three games to one, the Cavaliers rallied back to win.

This was the first championship in the Cleveland Cavaliers' forty-six-year history, fulfilling LeBron's draft day promise to bring a championship to his hometown.

2017   For the third straight year, the Golden State Warriors met the Cleveland Cavaliers in the NBA Finals with the Warriors winning this time. Led by newcomer and Finals MVP Kevin Durant, Golden State had one of the best postseason runs of all time, losing only once in the entire playoffs and regularly beating their opponents by double digits.

2018   For the first time in any of the four major sports, the same two teams met in the finals for four straight years. The Golden State Warriors once again beat the Cleveland Cavaliers, this time sweeping them 4–0, and Kevin Durant was named Finals MVP for the second year in a row.

2019   For the first time ever, a team from Canada won an NBA championship. Kawhi Leonard led the Toronto Raptors to a 4–2 series win over the Golden State Warriors, earning his second NBA Finals MVP Award. Leonard scored 732 points over the course of the playoffs, becoming only the third player in NBA history to score more than 730 points in one postseason.

Flagging the Fakes

These teams all have their own flags. But it looks like somebody has slipped a fake one in with the real ones. Can you spot them?

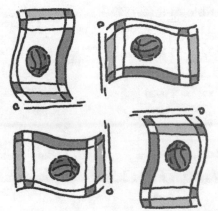

ACTIVITY
You can design your own flag. Get a rectangular piece of paper and some crayons. You could use a family crest, a pet portrait, or anything you like. Just have fun!

Europe has its own basketball teams. Can you pick them out from this jumble of letters?

Armani   Partizan
Barcelona   Prokom
Cibona   Real
Joventut   Unicaja
Olimpija

```
OLIMPIJACI
PLPARTIZAN
BARPRKUNCJ
REALKJOVDT
ARMANIOLIM
KOJOVENTUT
CIBONAANOB
BARCELONAB
PROKOMCAJO
OLIUNICAJA
```

Eight of the Top Teams in NBA History

Fans like to talk about their favorite teams—especially if their teams are highly successful. The ultimate sign of a successful team is one that has won multiple championships, either in consecutive years or during a particular era. Those teams are known as "dynasties" because they dominate the league during a certain period.

1966–1967 Philadelphia 76ers

The Sixers went 68–13, led by Wilt Chamberlain, Hal Greer, Chet Walker, and Billy Cunningham. Philadelphia started the season 46–4 and went on to set a record for most victories in a season (though that mark was eclipsed by the 1971–1972 Los Angeles Lakers). This memorable season also put an end to Boston's run of eight consecutive championships. The 76ers slammed the Celtics 4–1 in the Eastern Conference Finals before going on to down the San Francisco Warriors 4–2 in the 1967 NBA Finals.

1985–1986 Boston Celtics

Stung by a 4–2 loss to the Lakers in the 1985 Finals, Larry Bird led the Celtics to a 67–15 record with a team that featured Robert Parish, Kevin McHale, Dennis Johnson, Danny Ainge, and a rejuvenated Bill Walton. The team earned the best record in franchise history and a 4–2 defeat of Houston in the 1986 Finals. The Celtics had a 40–1 record at home, the best home-winning percentage (.976) in NBA history.

1986–1987 Los Angeles Lakers

During this 65–17 season, the Lakers reascended the NBA throne thanks to the high-flying, fast-break style of Magic Johnson, Kareem Abdul-Jabbar, James Worthy, Byron Scott, A.C. Green, and Michael Cooper. Magic averaged a career-best 23.9 points per game and led the league in assists with a 12.2 average. The Lakers defeated Boston 4–2 in the 1987 Finals after winning eleven of their first twelve games in the playoffs.

1995–1996 Chicago Bulls

Led by Michael Jordan, Scottie Pippen, and Dennis Rodman, this team set the NBA record for most wins in a single season, going 72–10 and winning each game by a whopping average of 12.3 points. This team was so dominant that they didn't lose back-to-back games until February and won eighteen games in a row at one point. In the 1995–1996 season, Jordan led the league in scoring and won the MVP award; Rodman led the league in rebounds; both Rodman and Pippen were named to the NBA All-Defensive First Team; and Phil Jackson, the coach of the Bulls, won Coach of the Year. Their dominance continued through the playoffs, when they lost only three games and beat the Seattle SuperSonics 4–2 to win the 1996 NBA Finals. This team still holds the record for highest winning percentage in the regular and postseason combined.

2007–2008 Boston Celtics

Kevin Garnett and Ray Allen, two of the best players in the league, joined Celtics star Paul Pierce to lead the Celtics to a 66–16 record and an NBA Championship. A year after finishing with the second-worst record in the NBA, the Celtics GM Danny Ainge completely changed the team, trading most of the Celtics' players to acquire the two perennial All-Stars. This team was defined by its dominant defense, holding teams to barely 90 points per game. Garnett was named the NBA's Defensive Player of the Year and Ainge won Executive of the Year. They faced off against their hated rivals, the L.A. Lakers, for the NBA Championship and beat them 4–2.

WORDS TO KNOW

Consecutive
Consecutive simply means in a row or without interruption. So if you won ten straight games, you won ten consecutive games.

Best-of-seven series
A best-of-seven series means the first team to win four games is declared winner of the series. While that can happen in as few as four games, the series can't go longer than seven games. Even if the teams are tied at three wins apiece after six games, the team who wins the next game will advance.

2012–2013 Miami Heat

Miami's "Big Three" of LeBron James, Dwyane Wade, and Chris Bosh helped this team get to a stellar record of 66–16. They had won the NBA Championship the year before, but now that they had played together for a couple of years, the trio really took off. At one point, they won twenty-seven games in a row, the second-longest streak in NBA history at the time. They faced the San Antonio Spurs in the Finals and beat them 4–3.

2013–2014 San Antonio Spurs

A year after losing to the Heat in the Finals, Tim Duncan, Tony Parker, and the rest of the Spurs went an NBA-best 62–20 in the regular season before dominating in the playoffs and winning the NBA Championship. This was a true team, with no one player averaging more than 17 points per game, but with six players averaging at least 10 points per game. This unselfish basketball helped the Spurs shut down the Heat in a rematch of the previous year, winning each game by an average of 14 points, the most in NBA Championship history.

2016–2017 Golden State Warriors

After winning an NBA record seventy-three games the year before (but losing the NBA Championship), the Warriors added Kevin Durant in free agency. Durant helped Steph Curry, Klay Thompson, and Draymond Green lead the team to a record of 67–15. This team was dominant in the regular season, with all four of their big stars being named to the All-Star Team. They won each of the first three playoff series without dropping a single game before winning the first three games of the NBA Finals against the Cleveland Cavaliers. They lost the next game but won the game after to finish the playoffs 16–1, the best record in NBA playoff history.

WORDS TO KNOW

Winning percentage
You can figure a team's winning percentage by dividing the number of games won by the number of games played. So if your team played four games and won three, you divide 3 by 4 and get a winning percentage of .750.

WORDS TO KNOW

Triangle offense
A sideline triangle is formed by the center in the low post, the forward standing on a wing, and a guard in one corner. The other guard is at the top of the key and the remaining forward in the high post, creating a two-man game. The spacing allows for passing, though the defense's reaction ultimately dictates what the offense does.

9

College Basketball and March Madness

The College Game Migrates West

The first intercollegiate basketball game was played on February 9, 1895. The Minnesota School of Agriculture defeated Hamline College 9–3. Less than a year later, the first college game was played with the current five-men-on-the-court format. The University of Chicago beat the University of Iowa in Iowa City 15–12. In Naismith's native Canada, McGill University beat Queen's University 10–6 in December 1902 in the first Canadian intercollegiate game.

By 1901, colleges such as Dartmouth, the University of Chicago, Columbia, Minnesota, Utah, Yale, and the Naval Academy started having men's games. That was just the beginning; by 1906, so many colleges and universities were playing basketball that conferences started to form.

Injuries occurred so frequently in the infancy of college basketball that President Theodore Roosevelt actually stepped in and suggested in 1910 that a governing body be formed to rule over the sport. This eventually evolved into the NCAA.

Women's basketball began in 1892 when Smith College hired physical education teacher Senda Berensen, who visited Dr. Naismith to learn more about the game of basketball. In 1893, Berensen had her Smith College freshmen and sophomores play each other in what is believed to be the first college women's game. She adapted the rules to better suit the women's game and published those in 1899. The first women's intercollegiate game was played in 1896. Stanford beat the University of California 2–1, and each team kept nine players at a time on the court.

March Madness

College basketball kept growing and growing through the years. While college football has the bowl season after the regular season, college basketball came up with a tournament all its own.

The NIT and NCAA Tournaments

In 1938, the Metropolitan Basketball Writers Association came up with the first college basketball tournament. They called it the National Invitation Tournament (NIT). Originally it had six teams, but over time it grew to include forty teams. Now it has thirty-two teams. The NCAA tournament was created in 1939. It started with eight teams and grew to sixty-eight. The NIT and NCAA tourneys of the 1930s really changed the dynamic of college basketball because the tournaments allowed teams from all over the country to face one another and determine the best team in the nation. The NIT and NCAA tournaments were actually viewed as equal events until the late 1970s.

In 1950, the City College of New York won both the NCAA tournament and the National Invitational Tournament.

TIP-IN

Though the NIT started out as a big deal, it is now the consolation prize for teams that do not make the 68-team NCAA tournament. Still, the NIT is a way for teams that didn't make the NCAA tourney to end the year on a high note, and it's always a treat for fans to see teams with good records battle each other.

Doing well in these tournaments helped teams recruit the best players. Some of the schools that did well in the early days of the tournaments are still powerhouses today, including UCLA, North Carolina, Duke, and Indiana. Kansas, whose program was started by Naismith himself, was another early powerhouse; it won its most recent NCAA title in 2008.

March Madness

Each spring, millions of people enjoy an incredible month of college basketball: the modern NCAA tournament. In the late 1970s, the NCAA tournament established itself as the premier event and the NIT took a back seat. Sixty-eight teams, ranked according to their strength, are invited to compete in the NCAA tournament. The top four teams receive a 1 seed, the next four strongest teams receive a 2 seed, and the ranking continues all the way down to the 16 seeds. Then the teams are divided into four regions of sixteen teams.

The tournament is set up so that the strongest seeds play the weakest seeds. The 1 seeds play the 16 seeds, the 2 seeds play the 15 seeds, and so on. This is why it's a big boost for a team to be a high seed; they face the teams with the weakest records who will probably be the easiest to beat. The team that loses is out of the tournament and the winner advances to the next round. Because of this format the tournament moves quickly. Thirty-six games of basketball are played in the first four days of the tournament; that's a total of 32 hours of basketball—if none of the games go into overtime!

If the tournament were set up perfectly, the higher-seeded team would always win and advance to the next round. In reality, this never happens. There are always upsets, and that's part of what makes watching the tournament so much fun. Every year people fill out brackets and try to predict when teams will win and lose. They compare their guesses with their friends and compete to see who can get the most right.

Confusing Recruits

This college team is recruiting new players by sending out an email, but it looks like some letters got mixed up on the way. Can you figure out what the message says? Here's a hint: the letters T, E, A, and M have been replaced with other letters.

Hollo Biskocbill Lovors,

Wo will bo visicing your cicy cho lisc Cuosdiy of chis ponch. Wo iro looking for sopo now playors. Copo ouc and soo if you iro good onough co join cho coip!

Koop shoocing!

—Cho Coich

RATING RECRUITS

"Blue chip" is the term used to describe a top player coming out of high school who is being recruited.

The Top NCAA Men's Teams of All Time

Certain colleges and universities are known for their legacies of strong basketball programs. UCLA, for example, has won a mindboggling eleven NCAA championships. But a few individual teams made such an impact on the game that they can be considered the best of all time.

1976 Indiana Hoosiers

The University of Indiana Hoosiers went 32–0 in 1976, the only Division I team that has ever gone undefeated. Led by coach Bobby Knight, the Hoosiers beat the defending champion UCLA Bruins in the Final Four and won the national championship in a game against their Big Ten rivals, the Michigan Wolverines. Indiana won its regular-season games by an average of more than 17 points a game and had two All-Americans in Scott May and Quinn Buckner.

1992 Duke Blue Devils

The 1992 Duke men's basketball team had superstars in Christian Laettner, Bobby Hurley, and Grant Hill, but they played as a team the whole season. They were the defending national champions, and Mike Krzyzewski coached them to a 34–2 record in the regular season.

The top-seeded Blue Devils breezed through the NCAA tournament—until they ran into Rick Pitino's Kentucky Wildcats in the Elite Eight. The two teams battled their way into overtime and Duke trailed 103–102 with only 2.1 seconds remaining. Christian caught a long pass from Grant, dribbled once, turned to the basket, and hit a 17-foot jumper to put the Blue Devils ahead just as time ran out.

★ FUN FACTS ★

The movie *Hoosiers* is loosely based on the true story of a small-town high school team in Indiana that beat a big-city school for the state championship.

Duke eked out a three-point win over Indiana in the Final Four and then ran away with an anticlimactic championship game against the University of Michigan's much hyped freshmen starters, the Fab Five.

1996 Kentucky Wildcats

After losing to Duke in the 1992 Elite Eight, Rick Pitino led his Wildcats to a Final Four appearance in 1993. But his best team was the 1996 Wildcats, who went 34–2 and featured future first-round NBA picks Antoine Walker, Tony Delk, Walter McCarty, Derek Anderson, and Ron Mercer. The Wildcats were at their best in the NCAA tournament, winning their six tourney games by an average of more than 20 points each.

1982 North Carolina Tar Heels

The 1982 University of North Carolina team had players like Michael Jordan, Sam Perkins, and James Worthy. None of their opponents could figure out how to stop their powerful offense. The Tar Heels went 34–2 in the regular season and advanced to the national championship game against Georgetown. With 17 seconds remaining in the game, Michael launched a 17-foot jumper to clinch a 63–62 victory for the Tar Heels.

1974 North Carolina State Wolfpack

The 1974 North Carolina State Wolfpack went 30–1. It was led by highflying David Thompson, who would go on to star for the Denver Nuggets, and 5-foot-6-inch point guard Monte Towe. The Wolfpack could win any way needed, beating Maryland 103–100 for the Atlantic Coast Conference title and then taking down UCLA 80–77 in the NCAA semifinals before finishing it off with a 76–64 NCAA championship win over Marquette.

FUN FACTS

In the 1982 title game, future NBA rivals Michael Jordan and Patrick Ewing faced off against each other. Three years earlier, Magic Johnson's Michigan State Spartans defeated Larry Bird's Indiana State Sycamores in the most-watched title game ever. The Bird-Magic rivalry continued in the NBA, where they met in the Finals in 1984, 1985, and 1987.

1968 UCLA Bruins

John Wooden's 1968 UCLA team lost to the University of Houston in the middle of the season but came back to trounce the same team in the NCAA tournament—by 32 points. UCLA had Lew Alcindor, who averaged 26 points and 16 rebounds a game. The Bruins downed North Carolina 78–55 to win the NCAA tournament.

1972 UCLA Bruins

John's 1972 UCLA Bruins dominated the landscape like no other team, before or since. They earned a perfect 30–0 record and beat opponents by an average of more than 32 points per game during the regular season. The team featured future NBA Hall of Fame center Bill Walton, who would later claim he was "embarrassed" by his play as UCLA beat Florida State by five, 81–76, in the NCAA championship game that year.

The Greatest College Players

Some of the greatest college players went on to become NBA superstars. Others didn't find as much success in the NBA, but fans still remember their biggest collegiate moments.

Lew Alcindor (Kareem Abdul-Jabbar)

Lew Alcindor, later Kareem Abdul-Jabbar, won three consecutive championships at UCLA in 1967, 1968, and 1969. Freshmen were not allowed to play on varsity, but Lew was so dominating he led the freshmen team past the UCLA varsity, which was ranked No. 1 in the nation at the time. He was named NCAA tournament Most Valuable Player all three years he was eligible and was the first winner of the Naismith College Player of the Year award in 1969.

TIP-IN

Kareem owns eight UCLA records, including most field goals (943), most points in a season (870), and most points in a single game (61).

College Copies

There are a lot of college basketball players with very similar skills. Sometimes they're so close it's hard to tell them apart! Can you see the 10 differences here?

Why did the chicken cross the basketball court?
He heard the referee calling fowls!

Bill Russell

Bill Russell would go on to become one of the great players of all time, but coming out of high school he only got one letter recruiting him. It was from a local school, the University of San Francisco. Bill arrived as a diamond in the rough and immediately became a defensive standout. He led San Francisco to fifty-five straight wins, including the 1955 and 1956 national championships.

Bill Bradley

Though he originally committed to Duke, Bill Bradley opted instead to go to Princeton University for an Ivy League education. The 6-foot-5-inch Bill was a three-time All-American and scored 58 points in an NCAA tournament win over Wichita State in 1965. Bill went on to become a US senator and was a candidate for the Democratic presidential nomination.

Pete Maravich

Louisiana State University had a scorer in Pete Maravich. No one had scored more points than Pete when he left college with 3,667 points, despite the fact that he'd only played three years because freshmen were not eligible. In eighty-three college games, Pete averaged 44.2 points a game and led the NCAA in scoring three times.

Jerry West

Jerry West put the eyes of the nation on West Virginia when he played for the Mountaineers, leading the team to the 1959 NCAA finals as a junior and earning the tournament's MVP award—even though his team lost. He played from 1958–1960, and in his final year averaged 29.3 points and 16.5 rebounds a game and recorded 134 assists for the season.

Elvin Hayes

Elvin Hayes was one of the first African-American players for the University of Houston. Elvin led Houston to the NCAA Final Four in 1967, scoring 25 points and grabbing 24 rebounds in a semifinal loss to eventual champ UCLA. The following year, Houston and UCLA played each other in the first nationally televised college basketball game, in which Elvin scored 39 points, recorded 15 rebounds, and kept Lew Alcindor to just 15 points.

Jerry Lucas

Jerry Lucas turned down basketball powerhouse Kentucky to go to Ohio State University; he was from nearby Middletown and earned an academic scholarship to Ohio State. The Buckeyes went 78–6 in his three years of varsity play. Jerry directed Ohio State to three finals, including the national championship in 1960, and became the only player to ever score 30 points and have 30 rebounds in the same game.

Christian Laettner

Christian Laettner will always be known for his buzzer-beating shot from the top of the key to beat Kentucky in the 1992 NCAA East Regional. Christian played in four consecutive Final Fours for Duke University and still has the record of having played in twenty-three NCAA tournament games. He owns the records in the NCAA tournament for most points scored (407) and most free throws made (142).

Team Effort

Here's a new team, but it doesn't have a name yet. Can you figure out which is the correct one? It must have:

- at least one S
- at least one I
- at least one B
- only one word with two syllables

Dribble Kings

Leapin' Lizards

Hoop Hogs

Basket Masters

Passing Princes

Jumping Giants

WORDS TO KNOW

Win streak
A win streak is how many victories in a row a team has. A losing streak is the number of defeats in a row a team has suffered.

David Thompson

David Thompson led North Carolina State to a perfect 27–0 season in 1973 when the team was not eligible for the NCAA tournament. The next year, he came back and led the Wolfpack to the NCAA title, beating defending champ UCLA. David and teammate Monte Towe are largely credited with inventing the alley-oop, where the ball is passed to someone in mid-flight and dunked. Called an idol by no less than Michael Jordan, David's jersey number 44 is the only one retired by NC State.

Oscar Robertson

Oscar Robertson averaged 33.8 points per game at the University of Cincinnati, the third highest in college history. In three varsity seasons, Cincinnati was 79–9 and made the Final Four twice. Oscar set nineteen school records and fourteen NCAA records.

Bill Walton

Bill Walton was a big force for UCLA from 1971 to 1974, leading the team to back-to-back NCAA titles in 1972 and 1973. In the 1973 title game win over Memphis, Bill made 21 of 22 shots from the field and scored 44 of UCLA's 87 points, which is widely regarded as the best single-game title performance of all time. Bill was also a key figure during UCLA's record eighty-eight-game win streak.

Glossary of Terms

Air ball
A shot that does not hit the rim; misses everything.

Alley-oop
A pass made to a teammate who catches the ball midflight and slam-dunks the ball into the hoop. A spectacular and crowd-pleasing play.

Alternate possessions
In college and high school, this rule substitutes for a jump ball during the game only (not at the start of the game). So if two players have possession of the ball at the same time—both have hands on it—the referee will blow the whistle. The official scorer keeps track with an arrow at courtside that shows whose turn it is to have possession, and it rotates back and forth. So the team that is awarded possession the first time will not get it the second time, but will get it the third time, and so on.

Arc
The trajectory of a shot; the three-point line is also called the three-point arc.

Assist
A pass that sets up a successful basket. The player who made that pass is credited with an assist.

Backboard
The glass, metal, or synthetic board the hoop is bolted to. It can also be used to bank in shots from the outside, on layups, or on free throws.

Backscreen
An offensive player moves away from the basket to set a screen for a teammate who either has the ball or is trying to get free for a pass.

Ball fake
Used to distract opponents, it can be a fake pass or shot.

Ball handler
The player who has the basketball; usually moving the ball up the court, it is the point guard.

Ball hog
Someone who does not pass the ball to teammates and takes most of the shots.

Bang the boards
A term used for trying hard to get rebounds; also called "crashing the boards."

Bank shot
A ball that goes off the backboard into the hoop. The backboard is thus used to "bank" the ball into the hoop by knowing right where to bounce it off the backboard so it goes into the hoop.

Baseball pass
A pass thrown with one hand.

Baseline
The line that runs the width of the court behind each basket that signifies out of bounds.

Basket interference
Touching the basketball while it is in any part of the "cylinder" or on the rim of the basket, reaching through the basket to touch the ball, or pulling down on the rim as an illegal defensive maneuver.

Behind-the-back pass
A pass made to a teammate by pushing the ball around your body behind your back.

Block
A shot that is knocked away.

Bounce pass
Bouncing the ball on the floor, usually once, while making a pass to a teammate.

Box out
Putting your body between an opponent and the basket to keep him from getting rebounds.

Brick

A shot that misses badly by clanking hard or awkwardly off the rim or backboard.

Buzzer beater

A shot that goes in just before time expires.

Carrying

When a player dribbling the ball temporarily stops and then continues. In effect, it is traveling and is similar to a double dribble.

Catch and face

The term used to get a pass and square up to the basket to shoot, done in one motion to allow the defender no time to react.

Center

The tallest player on the team, counted on to score baskets from in close, to win jump balls, block opposing players' shots, and get a lot of rebounds.

Charge

When an offensive player runs into a defender whose feet are planted.

Charity stripe

A nickname for the free-throw line.

Chest pass

A two-handed pass thrown from the chest.

Clear out

Offensive player or players moving out of an area so a teammate with the ball can try to move toward the basket.

Crossover dribble

Dribbling from one hand to the other; can be used to fake defenders about what direction the ball handler wants to go.

Cut

An offensive move often toward the basket or an open spot on the court to get away from a defender.

Cylinder

The area above the rim; once the ball enters that area it cannot be touched or it is goaltending.

Defensive rebound

If your opponent misses a shot and you get the ball it is a defensive rebound because it came at the end of the court you are defending.

Double-double

When a player has double figures (10 or more) in points and rebounds.

Double dribbling

When a player is dribbling the ball then stops, and then starts again. The other team gets possession of the ball.

Double team

When two defenders guard a single player to prevent him from getting the ball or scoring.

Dribbling

Bouncing the ball up and down—required to move with the basketball.

Driving

Dribbling the ball toward the basket.

Fadeaway jumper

Jumping backward at a slight angle while taking a shot. It is very hard to block.

Fast break

Moving the ball quickly up the court and not allowing defensive players to set up. Often results in outnumbering the defensive team momentarily if done fast, allowing a player an open or unguarded attempt to score.

Field goal

Any shot other than a free throw.

Field goal percentage

The number of shots (not including free throws) made divided by the number attempted. So if you took four shots and made two, you'd have a field goal percentage of 50.

Finger roll

Not as popular as it was in the 1980s, this involves scoring a "lay-in" or layup by letting the ball roll off the fingers.

GLOSSARY OF TERMS

Five-second violation

When inbounding the ball, the player trying to do it has to pass the ball inbounds within 5 seconds or the opposing team gets possession.

Flagrant foul

A foul made on purpose with too much physical contact or force, resulting either in automatic free throws or the player being thrown out of the game.

Flex offense

An offensive scheme designed in the 1970s that involves a lot of motion, screens, and cuts in the offense. Though it is considered too predictable to be used in the pros or even college, the plays are easy to remember and involve all players, so it is still used in kids' leagues as a way to teach basic skills.

Flop

A player exaggerates being contacted by an opposing player to try to get the referee to call a foul.

Foul

Illegal contact with an opponent: reaching in for a ball, jumping over a player's back for a rebound, running into a player trying to score if his feet are planted, or if the defender is moving when the collision occurs are some.

Foul line

The line 15 feet in front of the basket where free throws are attempted.

Foul out

Depending on the level of play, five or six fouls result in the player no longer being allowed to play in that particular game.

Four corners

A type of offense where players form a square in the offensive end while the player dribbling the ball is in the middle. By using screens and cuts, the team is trying to get a good shot attempt or layup.

Free throw

Shots taken after a foul by the opposing team. The game is stopped and the player is allowed to shoot one, two, or as many as three uncontested free throws, which are always worth 1 point each.

Free-throw percentage

The number of free throws made divided by free throws attempted. A good free-throw shooter makes at least seven or eight out of ten, and some players in the NBA make at least 90 percent of their free throws.

Full-court press

Using defensive pressure to cover the team with the ball the whole length of the court, from the time they inbound it all the way to the offensive end of the court.

Garbage time

When the outcome of the game is already decided because a team leads by an undefeatable amount of points and not enough time is left for the losing team to catch up. This is when coaches "clear the bench" and put in mostly substitutes.

Give and go

An offensive play where the player with the ball passes to a teammate and then cuts or otherwise takes off toward the hoop and gets the ball right back.

Goaltending

When the ball is on a downward arc into the basket or on the rim and is interfered with by a defender and the offensive team is awarded points whether the ball goes in or not.

Hook shot

Most often done by centers, though occasionally done by other players, when the player is perpendicular to the basket and sweeps the ball toward the basket in a hook motion, making it hard to defend or block.

Inbounds pass

The team with the ball has one player stand out of bounds and that player tries to pass it to one of her four teammates on the court.

Jump ball

The ball is tossed in the air and the best jumpers or tallest players from each team jump and try to tip it to a teammate; used to start a game.

☆ *133* ☆

Jump shot

Used with a field goal; the player jumps, usually straight up, as part of the shooting motion so that a defender cannot block the shot. This replaced the set shot.

Key

The shaded rectangular area in front of each basket that goes out to the foul line, shooting line, and half-circle where players stand to shoot free throws. In international basketball, the lane is shaped more like a trapezoid.

Lane violation

During a free-throw attempt, entering the lane too early, before the ball has hit the rim. The lane is the shaded area in front of the free-throw line.

Layup

A 2-point shot made from in close from either side of the basket, banked off the glass and into the basket. One of the most successful shots attempted if the player is open; however, it is also often blocked by taller players. Though often done off a fast break, it can also be done when a player becomes open near the basket.

Man-to-man defense

Each player guards another player on the opposing team, following that player everywhere on defense and trying to keep that player from receiving passes or taking shots.

Matchup zone

A combination of a zone defense and man-to-man defense. Defensive players match up with specific offensive players, while other defenders play zone and are responsible not for certain players but particular areas and guard only players who enter the zone they are responsible for.

Mikan drill

A popular drill at tryouts, preseason practices, and basketball camps. Standing under the basket, the player makes a layup with the right hand and catches the ball after it comes through the hoop and net with the left hand. Then the player makes a layup with the left hand and catches the ball with the right hand. Named after one of the NBA's first dominant big men, George Mikan.

Motion offense

Uses player movement to move the defense around and get offensive players open to make baskets. Often it is used to single out a weakness of the defensive team or to best use one of the strengths of the offensive team. Heavily used to create shooting lanes or lanes to drive to the basket. Particularly effective against taller or slower opponents.

Net

The white nylon or mesh that hangs from the hoop. A ball "swishes" through the net if it is shot so precisely that it does not touch the rim, creating the term "Nothing but net" for a really good shot.

One and one

These are given for nonshooting fouls. If the player makes the first shot, he gets a second shot. If he misses the first one, the ball is live and in play.

Overtime

An extra period of time to play if the score is tied at the end of regulation play; also known as OT. Points scored in overtime count just as they would for any other time during the game.

Paint

The shaded area of the key in front of the free-throw line.

Pass

Using any kind of throw or chest pass to get the ball to a teammate.

Penetration

When a player dribbles the ball into the paint toward the basket.

Perimeter

The area outside the lane. Players who shoot from behind 15 feet are often called perimeter shooters and players who rarely go into the paint are called perimeter players.

GLOSSARY OF TERMS

Period

A quarter in a four-quarter game. A half is divided into two quarters each at the professional level. Any game that goes into overtime is called an overtime period.

Personal foul

Illegal contact with an opponent, ranging from pushing or putting hands on players to running into them.

Pick

Setting a screen for a teammate.

Pick-and-roll

A player sets a screen (also called a pick) for the ball handler, then the screen setter slips behind the defender to get a pass from the ball handler.

Pivot

Rotating your body around one planted foot kept in a stationary position. As long as that one foot stays planted, a player with the ball can pivot left or right, toward or away from the basket.

Point guard

The number-one spot on the floor, the player who dribbles the ball up the court and sets up the offense. Though there are now taller point guards, traditionally the point guard is smaller, has good knowledge of the game, and gets a lot of assists by finding the open teammate to set up baskets.

Points

These are used to keep score of the game. A free throw is worth 1 point, field goals (including layups and dunks) inside the three-point arc are good for 2 points, and baskets shot with both feet behind the three-point arc are awarded 3 points.

Post

The area on either side of the free-throw line. The low post is closer to the basket and the high post is closer to the free-throw line. Centers usually play in the low post.

Post up

Taking a position close to the basket, facing away from the basket, and getting between the defender and the teammate with the ball to create a passing lane to receive the ball.

Power forward

Referred to as the number-four spot. A power forward can rebound and play inside and has the size and strength to get a lot of offensive and defensive rebounds, but score a lot on offense.

Princeton offense

Princeton devised an offense to capitalize on its fast, smaller players. It uses constant motion, screens, backdoor passing, cuts, and a lot of hustle. Players are also required to know the fundamentals well and be "smart" or "thinkers" on the court. The backdoor pass is often used for easy layups as defenses get disoriented and drawn out of position by the Princeton offense.

Putback

Getting a rebound off a missed shot by a teammate and immediately putting it back in for a 2-point field goal. Also called garbage points because they come from picking up others' mistakes (missed shots) or trash.

Quadruple-double

Ten or more each from four of five of these categories: points, rebounds, assists, steals, and blocks.

Rebound

Getting the ball after it hits the rim on an unsuccessful shot on either the defensive or offensive end.

Reverse dribble

Changing direction while bouncing the ball.

Reverse pivot

The same as a pivot, only stepping backward with the nonstationary foot. This is used to take a shot or to draw in the defender so the offensive player can drive to the basket or draw a foul.

Screen

A move used to block a player to free up a ball handler or a player trying to get open to receive a pass or to attempt a shot. Also called a pick, it depends on timing and possession because a player who is moving while setting a screen can be called for a foul.

Shootaround
This is a casual practice where players shoot at one hoop in a halfcourt setting.

Shooting guard
The number-two spot on the floor; a guard who can shoot from the outside, especially three-pointers.

Shot clock
Used to speed up the pace of a game and prevent teams with a lead from stalling or running out the clock. Forces teams to take a shot that at least hits the rim (or goes in) within a set amount of time, usually 24 seconds or 30 seconds, but occasionally 35 depending on the level of play. If a team fails to take a shot that at least hits the rim in the allotted shot clock time, the whistle is blown and possession is turned over to the opposing team.

Sidelines
The longer lines on each side of the court that indicate where out-of-bounds and in-bounds are.

Sixth man
The player who is not among the five players to start the game, but is the first player off the bench to substitute into the game for one of the starting five. This became such an important role

that the NBA came up with an award for the best sixth man each season.

Slam dunk
A field goal worth 2 points, but is often exciting for fans as a player jumps up into the air and forces the ball through the hoop with his hand touching or grabbing the rim as the ball is forced in. This is also a hard shot to block. Abdul-Jabbar became so proficient at this that it was banned by the NBA for nine years from the late 1960s to mid-1970s and is a favorite of both fans and TV stations that show highlights.

Small forward
Usually bigger than the guards but smaller than traditional forwards, a player who is a good shooter, quick, and can drive to the basket with the ball.

Spin dribble
Turning around to "shake off" a defender or prevent a steal while bouncing the ball; used to change direction.

Squaring up
When a shooter's shoulders face the basket in preparation for a shot attempt.

Starting lineup
The five players who are on the floor to start the game.

Steal
When a defensive player, without fouling, successfully takes possession of the ball from the offensive player. Can

be done by taking the ball, batting or deflecting a pass to a teammate, or intercepting a pass.

Strong side
The side of the court where the ball is at that time. If the ball goes to the other side, that becomes the strong side.

Substitution
When a player from the bench is put in for a player on the court. This is done throughout the game, so substitutes are often themselves substituted out of the game.

Swing man
A player who can play the shooting guard position (two spot) or small forward position (three spot).

Technical foul
A foul called for technical reasons or unsportsmanlike conduct, whether it is arguing with referees, getting in the face of an opponent, or instigating a brawl; called when the ball is not in play.

Ten-second line
When the halfcourt line is used to enforce the team with the ball to move it from their defensive end to the offensive end within 8 seconds of getting possession for the NBA; 10 seconds for college.

Three-point field goal
Shot from behind the three-point arc, a field goal worth 3 points. In the

GLOSSARY OF TERMS

NCAA the arc is 20 feet 9 inches from the basket; in the NBA it is 23 feet 9 inches.

Three-point play

When the offensive player is fouled making a field goal and makes the 1-point free throw awarded for the defender's foul.

Three-second violation

Offensive players must move in and out of the shaded area in front of the free-throw line; failing to move in and out of the key, standing in it for 3 seconds or more, results in a turnover.

Timeout

Used by coaches to discuss strategy or to figure out a strategy if the opposing team has made several baskets in a row.

Tip-off

The jump ball at center court that starts a game. Often used in schedules or media reports as the "tip off" time for a game.

Top of the key

The area at the end of the free-throw circle and the only place to shoot a three-pointer facing the basket head on.

Transition

When a team quickly goes from defense to offense; a good opportunity to get uncontested layups or open outside shots after getting possession of the ball.

Trap

A defensive technique when at least two players swarm the player with the ball to force a turnover.

Traveling

Most commonly called when a player takes too many steps with the ball while not dribbling.

Triangle offense

A sideline triangle is formed by the center in the low post, the forward standing on a wing, and a guard in one corner. The other guard is at the top of the key and the remaining forward in the high post, creating a two-man game. The spacing allows for passing, though the defense's reaction and attempts to defend it is what dictates what the offense does. Though it is seen as too complex for younger players, this "path of least resistance" offense, once mastered, can create gaudy scoring numbers if operated with the right players.

Triple-double

Getting 10 or more points, rebounds, and assists.

Turnover

This can result from the offense having the ball stolen, from an intercepted pass or one thrown out of bounds, traveling, or getting called for an offensive foul. All of these result in the ball being turned over to the opposing team.

Walking

Another term used for traveling. If a coach sees an opposing player travel and the referee does not call it, the coach will call out, "He walked!"

Weak side

The side of the court without the ball.

Zone defense

Rather than have each player guard a player on the opposing team, players are responsible only for certain areas on the defensive end of the court. There are several variations on the zone and it is created to either counter an opposing team's strengths or to minimize a team's own weaknesses.

Resources

Movies

High School Hero, 1927
Campus Confessions, 1938
The Basketball Fix, 1951
Tall Story, 1960
Hoosiers, 1986
Blue Chips, 1994
Hoop Dreams, 1994
Annie O, 1995
Celtic Pride, 1996
Eddie, 1996
Space Jam, 1996
The 6th Man, 1997
Air Bud, 1997
Soul in the Hole, 1997
The Basket, 1999
Michael Jordan, An American Hero, 1999
New Jersey Turnpikes, 1999
Passing Glory, 1999
Finding Forrester, 2000
Crossing the Line, 2002
Something to Cheer About, 2002
Coach Carter, 2005
Glory Road, 2006
The Winning Season, 2009
Just Wright, 2010

Magazines

Dime
Includes feature stories on players, reviews of shoes, and updates on players.

ESPN The Magazine
A fortnightly magazine designed for everything related to sports; especially during the college and professional basketball seasons, it has a lot of information on college and NBA basketball. Has a digital/online edition as well.

Slam
A comprehensive basketball magazine that began publishing in 1994 that combines hip-hop culture with basketball and includes a letters-to-the-editor section called "Trash Talk."

Sports Illustrated Kids (also known as Sports Illustrated for Kids)
Monthly magazine covering major sports including basketball. Also has a companion website, www.sikids.com, which includes puzzles, information about teams, games, and sports trivia. *Sports Illustrated Kids* is the kids' version of the popular adult sports magazine *Sports Illustrated*, both published by media giant Time Inc.

Websites

HoopsVibe.com
Has an NBA Gossip and Rumors section updated throughout the day, blogs, reviews of basketball shoes, and other items. www.hoopsvibe.com

InsideHoops.com
Has constantly updated news headlines, player movements, and other breaking news from professional and college basketball. www.insidehoops.com

NBA.com
The official source of news, features, and statistics for the NBA. You can find anything related to the NBA on this site, from schedules for this year to standings and biographies of current and former players. www.nba.com

WNBA.com
The official website for statistics, team information, and news for the WNBA (Women's National Basketball Association). Includes information on the teams, schedules, and how to buy tickets. www.wnba.com

Puzzle Answers

CHAPTER 1: PLAYING THE GAME
Name That Position • page 8

Shooting guard (usually the best scorer on the team)

Small forward (usually the most athletic)

Center (usually tallest and slowest)

Power forward (usually not as tall as the center)

Point guard (usually shortest and fastest)

Same but Different • page 20

Play Ball • page 27

Able, Ale, All, An, Ant, Ante, At, Ate, Bale, Ball, Ballet, Bane, Bat, Be, Bean, Beat, Bell, Belt, Ben, Bent, Bet, Blat, Bleat, Eat, Lab, Labe, Lane, Late, Lean, Leant, Lent, Let, Neat, Net, Tab, Table, Tale, Tall, Tan, Tea, Teal, Tell, Ten

Lists of Lists • page 28

Sports with the letter B in them: baseball, ballooning, handball, badminton, bungee jumping, basketball, T-ball, powerboating, racquetball, snowboarding

Sports equipment: shoulder pads, knee pads, helmet, goggles, flippers, skip rope, wrist guard, baseball bat, catcher's mitt, ski pole

Cities that have hosted the Olympics: Los Angeles, Innsbruck, Beijing, Atlanta, Nagano, Barcelona, Seoul, Sydney, Turin, Calgary

Sports where you don't kick a ball: hockey, golf, diving, tennis, lacrosse, squash, swimming, water polo, ultimate Frisbee, skiing

CHAPTER 2: HISTORY OF THE GAME
Lucky 13 • page 35

1. Opening an umbrella indoors
2. Putting shoes on the table
3. Letting a black cat cross your path
4. Walking under a ladder
5. Stepping on a crack

Do What Coach Says • page 39

⅔ will get on the team (8 out of 12)

Inflated Basketball • page 41

$20 = $560 $32 = $896
$27 = $756 $50 = $1,400

CHAPTER 3: GREAT PLAYERS OF YESTERDAY
Court Count • page 47

Point Well Taken • page 55

Bounce Back • page 58

React	Remote
Reposition	Recline
Return	Remodel

CHAPTER 4: GREAT PLAYERS OF TODAY
Matching Sets • page 61

Score! • page 72

OBASTALBLCSKRE

TKELSBCERALBOS

OCASSTABLLEEBKE

RALOKESCCASTBLE

KCLEOASBABSLRET

ALTLSBRSSEOAECK

KBSABCSLELEROAT

Opposites Attract • page 73

win/lose	professional/amateur
run/walk	player/worker
best/worst	tall/short
average/extraordinary	push/pull
major/minor	

CHAPTER 5: WOMEN'S BASKETBALL

Three's a Charm • **page 80**

15 times

Pick Up the Pieces • **page 83**

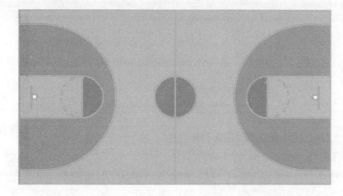

Amazing Athletes • **page 87**

```
C H E R Y L M I L L E R
        I
        S U E B I R D
        A
N A N C Y L I E B E R M A N
        E
S H E R Y L S W O O P E S
        L
        I
    R E B E C C A L O B O
T A M I K A C A T C H I N G S
```

Tally Ho! • **page 88**

20 + 40 + 10 + 3 = 73

25 + 25 + 15 + 6 = 71

34 + 10 + 8 + 10 + 10 = 72

11 + 11 + 11 + 11 + 25 = 69

1 + 1 + 60 + 3 + 13 = 78

22 + 22 + 22 + 10 = 76

9 + 9 + 9 + 27 + 26 = 80

16 + 10 + 10 + 10 + 10 + 23 = 79

CHAPTER 6: COACHES

Follow the Rules! • **page 91**

Everybody Chant • page 93

The game is on, it's getting late
The score's close, 87 to 88
It's up to you to decide their fate!
Make us proud of our state;
Let's tell the players we think they're great!

Crazy Coach • page 95

Run round robin regularly
Don't dribble downtown
Perfect players play politely
Tonight tall teams take turns
Grateful guards get goals

CHAPTER 7: HALL OF FAME
Lost in a Crowd • page 102

Double Duty • page 104

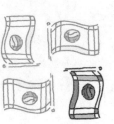

CHAPTER 8: THE NBA FINALS
Tag Team • page 108

Boston Celtics	Houston Rockets	Detroit Pistons
Chicago Bulls	Atlanta Hawks	Orlando Magic
Los Angeles Lakers	Toronto Raptors	New York Knicks
Miami Heat	Oklahoma City Thunder	

Flagging the Fakes • page 115

PUZZLE ANSWERS

Around the World • page 116

OLIMPIJA
  PARTIZAN

REAL
ARMANI
  JOVENTUT
CIBONA
BARCELONA
PROKOM
  UNICAJA

CHAPTER 9: COLLEGE BASKETBALL AND MARCH MADNESS
Confusing Recruits • page 123

Hello Basketball Lovers,
We will be visiting your city the last Tuesday of this month. We are looking for some new players. Come out and see if you are good enough to join the team!

Keep shooting!
—The Coach

College Copies • page 127

Team Effort • page 129
Dribble Kings

GET IN THE GAME WITH
EVERYTHING KIDS'!

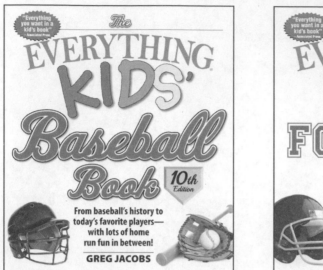
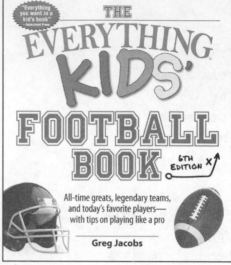
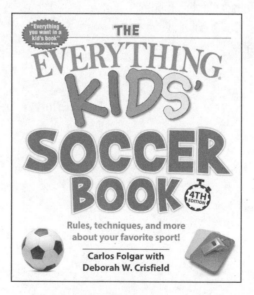